FINDING FLOW

The MasterMinds series:

These concise and accessible books present cutting-edge ideas by leading thinkers in a highly readable format, each title a crystallization of a lifetime's work and thought.

Other books in the MasterMinds series include:

After God: The Future of Religion by DON CUPITT

Extraordinary Minds by HOWARD GARDNER

Machine Beauty: Elegance and the Heart of Computing by DAVID GELERNTER

Future contributors include:

STEWART BRAND

JOHN MADDOX

JOHN SEARLE

SHERRY TURKLE

Praise for BasicBooks' Science Masters series:

"This is good publishing. PBS, eat your heart out."
—*Kirkus Reviews*

"Aimed at busy, nonmathematical readers, this precise series evinces solid quality control and begins under highly favorable auspices."
—*A. L. A. Booklist*

"If this standard is maintained, the Science Masters series looks set to play a major role in the responsible popularization of sciences."
—*New Scientist*

FINDING FLOW

THE PSYCHOLOGY OF ENGAGEMENT WITH EVERYDAY LIFE

MIHALY CSIKSZENTMIHALYI

BasicBooks
A Subsidiary of Perseus Books, L.L.C.

FIRST EDITION

Designed by Elliott Beard

Library of Congress Cataloging-in-Publication Data

Csikszentmihalyi, Mihaly.
    Finding flow in everyday life / by Mihaly Csikszentmihalyi.
— 1st ed.
        p.   cm. — (MasterMinds)
    Includes bibliographical references and index.
    ISBN 0-465-04513-8
    1. Happiness.   2. Conduct of life.   I. Title.   II. Series.
BF575.H27C848   1997
158—dc21   97-2008

97 98 99 00 ❖/RRD10 9 8 7 6

⇛CONTENTS

⹀ACKNOWLEDGMENTS

The results discussed in this book are based on research supported by the Spencer Foundation and the Alfred P. Sloan Foundation. A great number of colleagues and students have given invaluable help in the investigation of flow. I would like to thank especially Kevin Rathunde at the University of Utah; Samuel Whalen at Northwestern University; Kiyoshi Asakawa at Shikoku-Gakuen University in Japan; Fausto Massimini and Antonella Delle Fave at the University of Milan, Italy; Paolo Inghilleri at the University of Perugia, Italy; and at my own University of Chicago Wendy Adlai-Gail, Joel Hektner, Jeanne Nakamura, John Patton, and Jennifer Schmidt.

Of the many colleagues whose friendship has been such an invaluable support I want to give special thanks to Charles Bidwell, William Damon, Howard Gardner, Geoffrey Godbey, Elizabeth Noelle-Neumann, Mark Runco, and Barbara Schneider.

The Structures of Everyday Life

If we really want to live, we'd better start at once to try;
If we don't, it doesn't matter, but we'd better start to die.
                                        —W. H. Auden

The lines by Auden reproduced above compress precisely what this book is about. The choice is simple: between now and the inevitable end of our days, we can choose either to live or to die. Biological life is an automatic process, as long as we take care of the needs of the body. But to live in the sense the poet means it is by no means something that will happen by itself. In fact everything conspires against it: if we don't take charge of its direction, our life will be controlled by the outside to serve the purpose of some other agency. Biologically programmed instincts will use it to replicate the genetic material we carry; the culture will make sure that we use it to propagate its values and institutions; and other peo-

1

ple will try to take as much of our energy as possible to further their own agenda—all of this without regard to how any of this will affect us. We cannot expect anyone to help us live; we must discover how to do it by ourselves.

So what does "to live" mean in this context? Obviously, it doesn't refer simply to biological survival. It must mean to live in fullness, without waste of time and potential, expressing one's uniqueness, yet participating intimately in the complexity of the cosmos. This book will explore ways of living in this manner, relying as much as possible on findings in contemporary psychology and my own research, as well as on the wisdom of the past, in whatever form it was recorded.

I will reopen the question of "What is a good life?" in a very modest fashion. Instead of dealing in prophecies and mysteries I will try to stay as close to reasonable evidence as possible, focusing on the mundane, the everyday events that we typically encounter throughout a normal day.

A concrete example may illustrate best what I mean by leading a good life. Years ago my students and I studied a factory where railroad cars were assembled. The main workplace was a huge, dirty hangar where one could hardly hear a word because of the constant noise. Most of the welders who worked there hated their jobs, and were constantly watching the clock in anticipation of quitting time. As soon as they were out of the factory they hurried to the neighborhood saloons, or took a drive across the state line for more lively action.

Except for one of them. The exception was Joe, a barely literate man in his early sixties, who had trained himself to understand and to fix every piece of equipment in the factory, from cranes to computer monitors. He loved to take on machinery that didn't work, figure out what was wrong with it, and set it right again. At home, he and his wife built a large rock garden on two empty lots next to their house, and in it he built misty fountains that made rainbows—even at night. The hundred or so welders who worked at the same plant respected Joe, even though they couldn't quite make him out. They asked his help whenever there was any problem. Many claimed that without Joe the factory might just as well close.

Throughout the years I have met many CEOs of major companies, powerful politicians, and several dozen Nobel Prize–winners—eminent people who in many ways led excellent lives, but none that was better than Joe's. What makes a life like his serene, useful, and worth living? This is the crucial question this book will address. Three main assumptions underlie my approach. The first is that prophets, poets, and philosophers have gleaned important truths in the past, truths that are essential for our continued survival. But these have been expressed in the conceptual vocabulary of their time, so that to be useful, their meaning has to be rediscovered and reinterpreted every generation. The sacred books of Judaism, Christianity, Islam, Buddhism, and the Veda are the best repositories of the ideas that mattered most to our ancestors, and to ignore them is an act of childish conceit. But it is equally naive to believe that whatever was written down in the past contains an absolute truth that lasts forever.

The second plank on which this book is built is that currently science provides the most vital information to humankind. Scientific truth is also expressed in terms of the worldview of the times, and therefore will change and might be discarded in the future. There is probably as much superstition and misunderstanding embedded in modern science as there was in the old myths, but we are too close in time to tell the difference. Perhaps eventually ESP and spiritual energy will lead us to immediate truth without the need for theories and laboratories. But shortcuts are dangerous; we cannot delude ourselves that our knowledge is further along than it actually is. For better or for worse, at this time science is still the most trustworthy mirror of reality, and we ignore it only at our peril.

The third assumption is that if we wish to understand what real "living" entails, we should listen to the voices of the

past, and integrate their messages with the knowledge that
science is slowly accumulating. Ideological gestures—such as
Rousseau's project of returning to nature, which was a pre-
cursor to the Freudian faith—are just empty posturing when
one has no idea what human nature is. There is no hope in
the past. There is no solution to be found in the present. Nor
will we be better off by jumping ahead into an imaginary future. The only path to finding out what life is about is a patient, slow attempt to make sense of the realities of the past
and the possibilities of the future as they can be understood
in the present.

Accordingly, in this book "life" will mean what we experience from morning to night, seven days a week, for about
seventy years if we are lucky, for even longer if we are very
fortunate. This might seem a narrow perspective when compared to the much more exalted views of life that myths and
religions have made us familiar with. But to turn Pascal's wa-
ger on its head, it seems that, when in doubt, the best strategy is to assume that these seventy or so years are our only
chance to experience the cosmos, and we should make the
fullest use of it. For if we don't, we might lose everything;
whereas if we are wrong and there *is* life beyond the grave,
we lose nothing.

What this life will amount to is in part determined by the
chemical processes in our body, by the biological interaction
among organs, by the tiny electrical currents jumping between
the synapses of the brain, and by the organization of information that the culture imposes on our mind. But the actual quality of life—what we do, and how we feel about it—will be
determined by our thoughts and emotions; by the interpretations we give to chemical, biological, and social processes.
Studying the stream of consciousness passing through the
mind is the province of phenomenological philosophy. My
work in the past thirty years has consisted in developing a systematic phenomenology that makes use of the tools of the social sciences—primarily psychology and sociology—in order

to answer the question: What is life like? And the more practical question: How can each person create an excellent life?

The first step in answering such questions involves getting a good grasp of the forces that shape what we *can* experience. Whether we like it or not, each of us is constrained by limits on what we can do and feel. To ignore these limits leads to denial and eventually to failure. To achieve excellence, we must first understand the reality of the everyday, with all its demands and potential frustrations. In many of the ancient myths, a person who wanted to find happiness, love, or eternal life, had to first travel through the netherworld. Before being allowed to contemplate the splendors of heaven, Dante had to wander through the horrors of hell so he could understand what kept us from entering the pearly gates. The same is true of the more secular quest we are about to begin.

Baboons who live in the African plains spend about one-third of their life sleeping, and when awake they divide their time between traveling, finding and eating food, and free leisure time—which basically consists in interacting, or grooming each other's fur to pick out lice. It is not a very exciting life, yet not much has changed in the million years since humans evolved out of common simian ancestors. The requirements of life still dictate that we spend our time in a way that is not that different from the African baboons. Give and take a few hours, most people sleep one-third of the day, and use the remainder to work, travel, and rest in more or less the same proportions as the baboons do. And as the historian Emmanuel Le Roy Ladurie has shown, in thirteenth century French villages—which were among the most advanced in the world at the time—the most common leisure pursuit was still that of picking lice out of each other's hair. Now, of course, we have television.

The cycles of rest, production, consumption, and interaction are as much a part of how we experience life as our senses—vision, hearing, and so forth—are. Because the nervous system is so constructed that it can only process a small amount of information at any given moment, most of what we can experience must be experienced serially, one thing after the other. It is often said of a rich and powerful man that "Like the rest of us, he must pull his trousers on one leg at a time." We can swallow only one bite, hear only one song, read one paper, have one conversation at a time. Thus the limitations on attention, which determines the amount of psychic energy we have for experiencing the world, provide an inflexible script for us to live by. Across time and in different cultures, what people do and for how long is astonishingly similar.

Having just said that in some important respects all lives are similar, one must hasten to recognize the obvious differences. A Manhattan stockbroker, a Chinese peasant, and a bushman of the Kalahari will play out the basic human script in ways that at first will seem to have nothing in common. Writing about Europe in the sixteenth to eighteenth centuries, the historians Natalie Zemon Davis and Arlette Farge comment: "Daily life unfolded within the frame of enduring gender and social hierarchies." This is true of all social groups we have knowledge of: How a person lives depends in large part on sex, age, and social position.

The accident of birth puts a person in a slot that greatly determines what sorts of experiences his or her life will consist of. A boy of six or seven years, born into a poor family in one of the industrial regions of England two hundred years ago, was likely to wake up around five in the morning, rush to the mill to service the clanking mechanical looms till sunset, six days a week. Often he would die of exhaustion before reaching his teens. A girl of twelve in the silk-making regions of France around the same time would sit next to a tub all day, dipping silkworm cocoons in scalding water to melt the sticky substance that held the threads together. She was likely to succumb to respiratory diseases as she sat in wet clothes from dawn to dusk, and her fingertips eventually lost all feeling from the hot water. In the meantime, the children of the nobility learned to dance the minuet and to converse in foreign languages.

The same differences in life-chances are still with us. What can a child born into an urban slum in Los Angeles, Detroit, Cairo, or Mexico City expect to experience during a lifetime? How is that going to differ from the expectations of a child born into an affluent American suburb, or a well-to-do Swedish or Swiss family? Unfortunately there is no justice, nor any rhyme or reason, in one person being born into a starving community, perhaps even with a congenital physical defect, while another starts life with good looks, good health, and a large bank account.

So while the main parameters of life are fixed, and no person can avoid resting, eating, interacting, and doing at least some work, humanity is divided into social categories that determine to a large extent the specific content of experience. And to make it all more interesting, there is, of course, the matter of individuality.

If we look out of a window in winter, we might see millions of identical snowflakes cavorting by. But if we took a magnifying glass and looked at the flakes separately, we would soon discover that they were not identical—in fact, that each had a shape that no other flake duplicated exactly. The same is true of human beings. We can tell quite a lot about what Susan will experience just by the fact that she is human. We can tell even more by knowing she is an American girl, living in a certain specific community, with parents of such and such an occupation. But after everything is said and done, knowing all the external parameters will not allow us to predict what Susan's life will be like. Not only because random chance might throw all bets off, but more importantly, because Susan has a mind of her own with which she can either decide to squander her opportunities, or conversely overcome some of the disadvantages of her birth.

It is because of this flexibility of human consciousness that a book such as this can be written. If everything was determined by the common human condition, by social and cultural categories, and by chance, it would be useless to reflect on ways to make one's life excellent. Fortunately there is enough room for personal initiative and choice to make a real difference. And those who believe this are the ones with the best chance to break free from the grip of fate.

To live means to experience—through doing, feeling, thinking. Experience takes place in time, so time is the ultimate scarce resource we have. Over the years, the content of experience will determine the quality of life. Therefore one of the most essential decisions any of us can make is about how one's time is allocated or invested. Of course, how we invest time is not our decision alone to make. As we have seen earlier, stringent constraints dictate what we should do either as members of the human race, or because we belong to a certain culture and society. Nevertheless, there is room for personal choices, and control over time is to a certain extent in our hands. As the historian E. P. Thompson noted, even in the most oppressive decades of the Industrial Revolution, when workers slaved away for more than eighty hours a week in mines and factories, there were some who spent their few precious free hours in literary pursuits or political action instead of following the majority into the pubs.

The terms we use in talking about time—budgeting, investing, allocating, wasting—are borrowed from the language of finance. Consequently some people claim that our attitude toward time is colored by our peculiar capitalist heritage. It is true that the maxim "Time is money" was a favorite of that great apologist of capitalism, Benjamin Franklin, but the equation of the two terms is certainly much older, and rooted in the common human experience, rather than in our culture alone. In fact it could be argued that it is money that gets its value from time, rather than the other way around. Money is simply the most generally used counter for measuring the time invested in doing or making something. And we value money because to a certain extent it liberates us from the constraints of life by making it possible to have free time to do in it what we want.

What, then, do people do with their time? Table 1 gives a general notion of how we spend the sixteen or so hours a day in which we are awake and conscious. The figures are by necessity approximate, because depending on whether a person is young or old, man or woman, rich or poor, vastly different patterns might result. But by and large, the numbers in the table can begin to describe what an average day in our society looks like. They are in many ways quite similar to those obtained by time budgets in other industrialized countries.

Table 1
Where Does Time Go?

Based on daytime activities reported by representative adults and teenagers in recent U.S. studies. Percentages will differ by age, gender, social class, and personal preference—minimum and maximum ranges are indicated. Each percentage point is equivalent to about one hour per week.

Productive Activities		Total: 24–60%
Working at work, or studying	20–45%	
Talking, eating, daydreaming while at work	4–15%	
Maintenance Activities		Total: 20–42%
Housework (cooking, cleaning, shopping)	8–22%	
Eating	3–5%	
Grooming (washing up, dressing)	3–6%	
Driving, transportation	6–9%	
Leisure Activities		Total: 20–43%
Media (TV and reading)	9–13%	
Hobbies, sports, movies, restaurants	4–13%	
Talking, socializing	4–12%	
Idling, resting	3–5%	

Sources: Csikszentmihalyi and Graef 1980; Kubey and Csikszentmihalyi 1990; Larson and Richards 1994.

What we do during an average day can be divided into three major kinds of activities. The first and largest includes what we must do in order to generate energy for survival and comfort. Nowadays this is almost synonymous with "making money," since money has become the medium of exchange for most things. However, for young people still in school, learning might be included among these *productive* activities, because for them education is the equivalent of adult work, and the first will lead into the second.

Between a quarter to more than half of our psychic energy goes into such productive activities, depending on the kind of job, and whether one works full or part time. Although most full-time workers are on the job about forty hours a week, which is 35 percent of the 112 waking hours of the week, the figure does not reflect reality exactly, because of the forty hours per week spent on the job workers actually work only about thirty, the remainder being spent in talking, daydreaming, making lists, and other occupations irrelevant to work.

Is this much time or little? It depends on what we compare it to. According to some anthropologists, among the least technologically developed societies, such as the tribesmen of the Brazilian jungles or the African deserts, grown men rarely spend more than four hours a day providing for their livelihood—the rest of the time they spend resting, chatting, singing, and dancing. On the other hand, during the hundred years or so of industrialization in the West, before the unions were able to regulate working time, it was not unusual for workers to spend twelve or more hours a day in the factory. So the eight-hour workday, which is currently the norm, is about halfway between the two extremes.

Productive activities create new energy; but we need to do a great deal of work just to preserve the body and its possessions. Therefore about a fourth of our day is involved in various sorts of *maintenance* activities. We keep the body in shape by eating, resting, grooming; our possessions by cleaning, cooking, shopping, and doing all sorts of housework.

Traditionally women have been burdened by maintenance work while men have taken on the productive roles. This difference is still quite strong in the contemporary U.S.: while men and women spend equal amounts of time eating (about 5 percent), women devote twice as much time as men do to all the other maintenance activities.

The gender-typing of household tasks is of course even more severe practically everywhere else. In the former Soviet Union, where gender equality was a matter of ideology, married women doctors and engineers still had to do all the housework in addition to their paying jobs. In most of the world, a man who cooks for his family or does the dishes loses his self-respect as well as the respect of others.

This division of labor seems to be as old as humanity itself. In the past, however, the maintenance of the household often required enormously strenuous labor from women. One historian describes the situation in Europe four centuries ago:

> Women carried water to steep mountain terraces in areas . . . where water was scarce. . . . They cut and dried turf, collected kelp, firewood, weeds by the roadside to feed rabbits. They milked cows and goats, grew vegetables, collected chestnuts and herbs. The commonest source of heating for British and some Irish and Dutch farmers was animal turds, which were gathered by hand by women and received their final drying out stacked near the family fire. . . .

Plumbing and electronic appliances have certainly made a difference in the amount of physical effort it takes to run a household, just as technology has eased the physical burden of productive work. But most women in Asia, Africa, and South America—in other words, most women in the world—still have to devote a major part of their lives to keeping the material and emotional infrastructure of their families from collapsing.

Time left over from productive and maintenance necessities is free time, or *leisure*, which takes up about another fourth of our total time. According to many past thinkers, men and women could only realize their potential when they had nothing to do. It is during leisure, according to the Greek philosophers, that we become truly human by devoting time to self-development—to learning, to the arts, to political activity. In fact the Greek term for leisure, *scholea*, is the root from which our word "school" comes from, since the idea was that the best use for leisure was to study.

Unfortunately this ideal is seldom realized. In our society free time is occupied by three major sorts of activities—none being quite up to what the Greek scholars, or men of leisure, had in mind. The first is media consumption—mostly television, with a sprinkling of newspaper and magazine reading. The second is conversation. The third is a more active use of free time, and therefore the closest to the old ideal: it involves hobbies, making music, doing sports and exercise, going to restaurants and movies. Each of these three major kinds of leisure takes at least four and as much as twelve hours each week.

Watching TV, which on the average takes up the most psychic energy of all leisure pursuits, is probably also the most novel form of activity in human experience. Nothing men and women have done so far during the millions of years of evolution has been as passive, as addictive in the ease with which it attracts attention and keeps hold of it—unless we count staring into space, taking a siesta, or going into a trance as the Balinese were wont to do. The apologists for the medium claim that all sorts of interesting information is provided by television. This is true, but as it is much easier to produce programs that titillate rather than elevate the viewer, what most people watch is unlikely to help in developing the self.

These three main functions—production, maintenance, and leisure—absorb our psychic energy. They provide the information that goes through the mind day after day, from birth to the end of life. Thus, in essence, what our life is consists in experiences related to work, to keeping things we already have from falling apart, and to whatever else we do in our free time. It is within these parameters that life unfolds, and it is how we choose what we do, and how we approach it, that will determine whether the sum of our days adds up to a formless blur, or to something resembling a work of art.

Everyday life is defined not only by what we do, but also by who we are with. Our actions and feelings are always influenced by other people, whether they are present or not. Ever since Aristotle it has been known that humans were social animals; both physically and psychologically we depend on the company of others. Cultures differ in terms of how much a person is influenced by others, or by the internalized opinion of others when they are alone. For example, traditional Hindu persons were not considered to be separate individuals as we think of them, but rather nodes in an extended social network. One's identity was determined not so much by one's unique thoughts and actions, but rather by whose child, sibling, cousin, parent one was. In our time also, compared to Caucasian children, those from East Asian backgrounds are much more aware of parental expectations and opinions even when they are alone—in psychoanalytic terms, we might say that they have a stronger superego. But no matter how individualistic a culture might become, other people still determine to a large extent the quality of a person's life.

Most people spend roughly equal amounts of time in three social contexts. The first is made up of strangers, coworkers, or—for young people—fellow students. This "public" space is where one's actions are evaluated by others, where one competes for resources, and where one might establish collaborative relationships with others. It has been argued that this public sphere of action is the most important for developing one's potential, the one where the highest risks are run but the greatest growth occurs.

The second context is made up of one's family—for children their parents and siblings, for adults their partners, spouses, and children. While recently the very notion of "family" as a recognizable social unit has been severely criticized, and while it is true that no one kind of arrangement fits this definition in time and space, it is also true that always and everywhere there has been a group of people with whom one reckoned special bonds of kinship, with whom one felt safer, and for whom one felt a greater sense of responsibility than for others. No matter how strange nowadays some of our reconstituted families are in comparison with an ideal nuclear family, close relatives still provide a unique kind of experience.

Then there is the context defined by the absence of other people—solitude. In technological societies we spend about one-third of the day alone, a much greater proportion than in most tribal societies, where being alone is often considered to be very dangerous. Even for us being alone is undesirable; the vast majority of people try to avoid it as much as possible. Although it is possible to learn to enjoy solitude, it is a rare acquired taste. But whether we like it or not, many of the obligations of daily life require for us to be alone: children have to study and practice by themselves, housewives take care of the home alone, and many jobs are at least in part solitary. So even if we don't enjoy it, it is important to learn to tolerate solitude, or else the quality of our lives is bound to suffer.

In this chapter and the next one, I talk about how people use their time, how much of it they spend alone or with others, and how they feel about what they do. What is the evidence on which such assertions are based?

The most prevalent way to find out about what people do with their time is through polls, surveys, and time budgets. These methods usually ask people to fill out a diary at the end of a day or a week; they are easy to administer, but because they are based on recollection, are not very precise. Another method is the Experience Sampling Method, or ESM, which I developed at the University of Chicago in the early seventies. The ESM uses a pager or a programmable watch to signal people to fill out two pages in a booklet they carry with them. Signals are programmed to go off at random times within two-hour segments of the day, from early morning to 11 P.M. or later. At the signal the person writes down where she is, what she is doing, what she is thinking about, who she is with, and then rates her state of consciousness at the moment on various numerical scales—how happy she is, how much she is concentrating, how strongly she is motivated, how high her self-esteem is, and so on.

At the end of a week, each person will have filled out up to fifty-six pages of the ESM booklet, providing a virtual film strip of his or her daily activities and experiences. We can trace a person's activities from morning to night day by day over the week, and we can follow his or her mood swings in relation to what the person does and who he is with.

At our Chicago laboratory, we have collected over the years a total of more than seventy thousand pages from about twenty-three hundred respondents; investigators at universities in other parts of the world have more than tripled these figures. Large numbers of responses are important because they allow us to look into the shape and quality of daily life in great detail and with considerable precision. It allows us to see, for example, how often people eat meals, and how they feel when they do so. Furthermore, we can see whether teenagers, adults, and old people feel the same way about meals, and whether eating is a similar experience when one eats alone or in company. The method also allows comparisons among Americans, Europeans, Asians, and any other culture where the method can be used. In what follows, I will be using results obtained by surveys and polls interchangeably with ESM results. The notes at the end of the book will indicate the sources from which the data were obtained.

The Content of Experience

We have seen that work, maintenance, and leisure take up most of our psychic energy. But one person might love work and the other hate it; one person might enjoy free time and the other be bored when there is nothing to do. So while what we do day in and day out has a lot to do with what kind of life we have, how we experience what we do is even more important.

Emotions are in some respect the most subjective elements of consciousness, since it is only the person himself or herself who can tell whether he or she truly experiences love, shame, gratitude, or happiness. Yet an emotion is also the most objective content of the mind, because the "gut feeling" we experience when we are in love, or ashamed, or scared, or happy, is generally more real to us than what we observe in the world outside, or whatever we learn from science or logic. Thus we often find ourselves in the paradoxical position of being like behavioral psychologists when we look at other people, discounting what they say and trusting only what they do; whereas when we look at ourselves we are like phenomenologists, taking our inner feelings more seriously than outside events or overt actions.

Psychologists have identified up to nine basic emotions that can reliably be identified by facial expressions among people living in very different cultures; thus it seems that just as all humans can see and can speak, so they also share a common set of feeling states. But to simplify as much as possible, one can say that all emotions share in a basic duality: they are either positive and attractive, or they are negative and repulsive. It is because of this simple feature that emotions help us choose what should be good for us. A baby is attracted to a human face, and is happy when she sees her mother, because it helps her bond with a caretaker. We feel pleasure when eating, or when with a member of the opposite sex, because the species would not survive if we didn't seek out food and sex. We feel an instinctive revulsion at the sight of snakes, insects, rotten smells, darkness—all things that in the evolutionary past might have presented serious dangers to survival.

In addition to the simple genetically wired emotions, humans have developed a great number of more subtle and tender, as well as debased, feelings. The evolution of self-reflective consciousness has allowed our race to "toy" with feelings, to fake or manipulate feelings in ways that no other animal can. The songs, dances, masks of our ancestors evoked dread and awe, joy and intoxication. Horror movies, drugs, and music do the same thing now. But originally emotions served as signals about the outside world; now they are often detached from any real object, to be indulged in for their own sake.

Happiness is the prototype of the positive emotions. As many a thinker since Aristotle has said, everything we do is ultimately aimed at experiencing happiness. We don't really want wealth, or health, or fame as such—we want these things because we hope that they will make us happy. But happiness we seek not because it will get us something else, but for its own sake. If happiness is really the bottom line of life, what do we know about it?

Until mid-century, psychologists were reluctant to study happiness because the reigning behaviorist paradigm in the social sciences held that subjective emotions were too flimsy to be proper subjects of scientific research. But as the "dust-bowl empiricism" in academia has cleared in the last few decades so that the importance of subjective experiences could again be recognized, the study of happiness has been pursued with renewed vigor.

What has been learned is both familiar and surprising. It is surprising, for instance, that despite problems and tragedies, all over the world people tend to describe themselves as much more happy than unhappy. In America, typically one-third of respondents from representative samples say that they are "very happy," and only one in ten that they are "not too happy." The majority rate themselves above the halfway mark, as "pretty happy." Similar results are reported from dozens of other countries. How can this be, when thinkers through the ages, reflecting on how short and painful life can be, have always told us that the world is a vale of tears, and we were not made to be happy? Perhaps the reason for the discrepancy is that prophets and philosophers tend to be per-fectionists, and the imperfections of life offend them. Whereas the rest of humankind is glad to be alive, imperfec-tions and all.

Of course there is a more pessimistic explanation, namely, that when people say they are pretty happy they are deceiv-ing either the researcher who is taking the poll, or more likely, they are whistling in the dark. After all, Karl Marx has accustomed us to think that a factory worker can feel he is perfectly happy, but this subjective happiness is a self-deception that means nothing because objectively the worker is alienated by the system that exploits his labor. Jean-Paul

Sartre has told us that most people live with "false consciousness," pretending even to themselves that they are living in the best of all possible worlds. More recently Michel Foucault and the postmodernists have made it clear that what people tell us does not reflect real events, but only a style of narrative, a way of talking that refers only to itself. While these critiques of self-perception illuminate important issues that have to be recognized, they also suffer from the intellectual arrogance of scholars who believe their interpretations of reality should take precedence over the direct experience of the multitude. The profound doubts of Marx, Sartre, and Foucault notwithstanding, I still think that when a person says he is "pretty happy," one has no right to ignore his statement, or interpret it to mean the opposite.

Another set of familiar yet surprising findings has to do with the relationship between material well-being and happiness. As one would expect, people who live in nations that are materially better off and politically more stable rate themselves happier (e.g., the Swiss and Norwegians say they are happier than Greeks and Portuguese)—but not always (e.g., the poorer Irish claim to be happier than the wealthier Japanese). But within the same society there is only a very weak relationship between finances and satisfaction with life; billionaires in America are only infinitesimally happier than those with average incomes. And while personal income in the U.S. more than doubled between 1960 and the 1990s in constant dollars, the proportion of people saying they are very happy remained a steady 30 percent. One conclusion that the findings seem to justify is that beyond the threshold of poverty, additional resources do not appreciably improve the chances of being happy.

A number of personal qualities are related to how happy people describe themselves to be. For instance, a healthy extrovert with strong self-esteem, a stable marriage, and religious faith will be much more likely to say he is happy than a chronically ill, introverted, and divorced atheist with low self-esteem. It is in looking at these clusters of relationships that the skepticism of the postmodernist critique might make sense. It is likely, for instance, that a healthy, religious person will construct a "happier" narrative about his or her life than one who is not, regardless of the actual quality of experience. But since we always encounter the "raw" data of experience through interpretive filters, the stories we tell about how we feel are an essential part of our emotions. A woman who says she is happy to work two jobs to keep a roof over her children's head is probably in fact happier than a woman who doesn't see why she should have to bother with even a single job.

But happiness is certainly not the only emotion worth considering. In fact, if one wants to improve the quality of everyday life, happiness may be the wrong place to start. In the first place, self-reports of happiness do not vary from person to person as much as other feelings do; no matter how empty a life otherwise might be, most persons will be reluctant to admit being unhappy. Furthermore, this emotion is more a personal characteristic than a situational one. In other words, over time some people come to think of themselves as happy regardless of external conditions, while others will become used to feeling relatively less happy no matter what happens to them. Other feelings are much more influenced by what one does, who one is with, or the place one happens to be. These moods are more amenable to direct change, and because they are also connected to how happy we feel, in the long run they might lift our average level of happiness.

For instance, how active, strong, and alert we feel depends a lot on what we do—these feelings become more intense when we are involved with a difficult task, and they get more attenuated when we fail at what we try to do, or when we don't try to do anything. So these feelings can be directly affected by what we choose to do. When we feel active and strong we are also more likely to feel happy, so that in time the choice of what we do will also affect our happiness. Similarly most people feel they are more cheerful and sociable when they are with others than when they are alone. Again, cheerfulness and sociability are related to happiness, which probably explains why extroverts on the average tend to be happier than introverts.

The quality of life does not depend on happiness alone, but also on what one does to be happy. If one fails to develop goals that give meaning to one's existence, if one does not use the mind to its fullest, then good feelings fulfill just a fraction of the potential we possess. A person who achieves contentment by withdrawing from the world to "cultivate his own garden," like Voltaire's *Candide*, cannot be said to lead an excellent life. Without dreams, without risks, only a trivial semblance of living can be achieved.

Emotions refer to the internal states of consciousness. Negative emotions like sadness, fear, anxiety, or boredom produce "psychic entropy" in the mind, that is, a state in which we cannot use attention effectively to deal with external tasks, because we need it to restore an inner subjective order. Positive emotions like happiness, strength, or alertness are states of "psychic negentropy" because we don't need attention to ruminate and feel sorry for ourselves, and psychic energy can flow freely into whatever thought or task we choose to invest it in.

When we choose to invest attention in a given task, we say that we have formed an intention, or set a goal for ourselves. How long and how intensely we stick by our goals is a function of motivation. Therefore intentions, goals, and motivations are also manifestations of psychic negentropy. They focus psychic energy, establish priorities, and thus create order in consciousness. Without them mental processes become random, and feelings tend to deteriorate rapidly.

Goals are usually arranged in a hierarchy, from trivial ones, like getting to the corner store to buy some ice cream, to risking one's life for the country. In the course of an average day, about one-third of the time people will say that they do what they do because they wanted to do it, one-third because they had to do it, and the last third because they had nothing better to do. These proportions vary by age, gender, and activity: children feel they have more choice than their fathers, and men more than their wives; whatever a person does at home is perceived to be more voluntary than at work.

Quite a bit of evidence shows that whereas people feel best when what they do is voluntary, they do not feel worst when what they do is obligatory. Psychic entropy is highest instead when persons feel that what they do is motivated by not having anything else to do. Thus both intrinsic motivation (wanting to do it) and extrinsic motivation (having to do it) are preferable to the state where one acts by default, without having any kind of goal to focus attention. The large part of life many people experience as being thus unmotivated leaves a great deal of room for improvement.

Intentions focus psychic energy in the short run, whereas goals tend to be more long-term, and eventually it is the goals that we pursue that will shape and determine the kind of self that we are to become. What makes Mother Theresa the nun radically different from Madonna the singer are the goals into which they have invested their attention throughout their lives. Without a consistent set of goals, it is difficult to develop a coherent self. It is through the patterned investment of psychic energy provided by goals that one creates order in experience. This order, which manifests itself in predictable actions, emotions, and choices, in time becomes recognizable as a more or less unique "self."

The goals one endorses also determine one's self-esteem. As William James pointed out over a hundred years ago, self-esteem depends on the ratio of expectation to successes. A person may develop low self-esteem either because he sets his goals too high, or because he achieves too few successes. So it is not necessarily true that the person who achieves most will have the highest self-esteem. Contrary to what one would expect, Asian-American students who get excellent grades tend to have lower self-esteem than other minorities who are academically less successful, because proportionately their goals are set even higher than their success. Mothers who work full-time have lower self-esteem than mothers who do not work at all, because although they accomplish more, their expectations still outpace their achievements. From this it follows that contrary to popular wisdom, increasing children's self-esteem is not always a good idea—especially if it is achieved by lowering their expectations.

There are other misconceptions concerning intentions and goals. For instance, some point out that Eastern religions, such as the various forms of Hinduism and Buddhism, prescribe the abolition of intentionality as a prerequisite for happiness. They claim that only by relinquishing every desire, by achieving a goalless existence, can we hope to avoid unhappiness. This line of thought has influenced many young people in Europe and America to attempt to reject all goals, in the belief that only completely spontaneous and random behavior leads to an enlightened life.

In my opinion this reading of the Eastern message is rather superficial. After all, to try abolishing desire is itself a tremendously difficult and ambitious goal. Most of us are so thoroughly programmed with genetic and cultural desires that it takes an act of almost superhuman will to still them all. Those who expect that by being spontaneous they will avoid setting goals, usually just follow blindly the goals set down for them by instincts and education. They often end up being so mean, lecherous, and prejudiced as to stand a good Buddhist monk's hair on end.

The true message of the Eastern religions, it seems to me, is not the abolition of all goals. What they tell us is that most intentions we form spontaneously are to be mistrusted. To make sure that we survive in a dangerous world dominated by scarcity, our genes have programmed us to be greedy, to want power, to dominate over others. For the same reason, the social group into which we are born teaches us that only those who share our language and religion are to be trusted. The inertia of the past dictates that most of our goals will be shaped by genetic or by cultural inheritance. It is these goals, the Buddhists tell us, that we must learn to curb. But this aim requires very strong motivation. Paradoxically, the goal of rejecting programmed goals might require the constant investment of all one's psychic energy. A Yogi or a Buddhist monk needs every ounce of attention to keep programmed desires from irrupting into consciousness, and thus have little psychic energy left free to do anything else. Thus the praxis of the religions of the East is almost the opposite of how it has usually been interpreted in the West.

Learning to manage one's goals is an important step in achieving excellence in everyday life. To do so, however, does not involve either the extreme of spontaneity on the one hand, or compulsive control on the other. The best solution might be to understand the roots of one's motivation, and while recognizing the biases involved in one's desires, in all humbleness to choose goals that will provide order in one's consciousness without causing too much disorder in the social or material environment. To try for less than this is to forfeit the chance of developing your potential, and to try for much more is to set yourself up for defeat.

The third content of consciousness are cognitive mental operations. Thinking is such a complex subject that it is entirely out of the question to deal with it systematically here—instead it makes sense to simplify the subject so that we can talk about it in relation to everyday life. What we call thinking is also a process whereby psychic energy gets ordered. Emotions focus attention by mobilizing the entire organism in an approach or an avoidance mode. Goals do it by providing images of desired outcomes. Thoughts order attention by producing sequences of images that are related to each other in some meaningful way.

For instance, one of the most basic mental operations consists in the linking of cause and effect. How this begins in a person's life can be easily observed when an infant first discovers that by moving her hand she can ring the bell hanging over the crib. This simple connection is the paradigm on which much of later thinking is based. With time, however, the steps from causes to effects become increasingly more abstract and removed from concrete reality. An electrician, a musical composer, a stockbroker consider simultaneously hundreds of possible connections between the symbols on which they are operating in their minds—watts and ohms, notes and beats, the buying and selling prices of stocks.

By now it is probably apparent that emotions, intentions, and thoughts do not pass through consciousness as separate strands of experience, but that they are constantly interconnected, and modify each other as they go along. A young man falls in love with a girl, and experiences all the typical emotions that love implies. He intends to win her heart, and begins to think of how to reach this goal. He figures that getting himself a snazzy new car will win the girl's attention. So now the goal of earning money to buy a new car becomes embedded in the goal of wooing—but having to work more may interfere with going fishing and produce negative emotions, which generate new thoughts, which in turn may bring the boy's goals in line with his emotions . . . the stream of experience always carries many such bits of information concurrently.

To pursue mental operations to any depth, a person has to learn to concentrate attention. Without focus, consciousness is in a state of chaos. The normal condition of the mind is one of informational disorder: random thoughts chase one another instead of lining up in logical causal sequences. Unless one learns to concentrate, and is able to invest the effort, thoughts will scatter without reaching any conclusion. Even daydreaming—that is, the linking together of pleasant images to create some sort of mental motion picture—requires the ability to concentrate, and apparently many children never learn to control their attention sufficiently to be able to daydream.

Concentration requires more effort when it goes against the grain of emotions and motivations. A student who hates math will have a hard time focusing attention on a calculus textbook long enough to absorb the information it contains, and it will take strong incentives (such as wanting to pass the course) for him to do so. Usually the more difficult a mental task, the harder it is to concentrate on it. But when a person likes what he does and is motivated to do it, focusing the mind becomes effortless even when the objective difficulties are great.

Generally, when the issue of thinking comes up, most people assume it must have to do with intelligence. They are interested in individual differences in thinking, such as: "What's my IQ?" or: "He is a genius at math." Intelligence refers to a variety of mental processes; for instance, how easily one can represent and manipulate quantities in the mind, or how sensitive one is to information indexed in words. But as Howard Gardner has shown, it is possible to extend the concept of intelligence to include the ability to differentiate and to use all kinds of information, including muscle sensations, sounds, feelings, and visual shapes. Some children are born with an above-average sensitivity to sound. They can discriminate tones and pitches better than others, and as they grow up they learn to recognize notes and produce harmonies more easily than their peers. Similarly small advantages at the beginning of life can develop into large differences in visual, athletic, or mathematical abilities.

But innate talents cannot develop into a mature intelligence unless a person learns to control attention. Only through extensive investments of psychic energy can a child with musical gifts turn into a musician, or a mathematically gifted child into an engineer or physicist. It takes much effort to absorb the knowledge and the skills that are needed to do the mental operations an adult professional is supposed to perform. Mozart was a prodigy and a genius, but if his father hadn't forced him to practice as soon as he was out of diapers, it is doubtful his talent would have blossomed as it did. By learning to concentrate, a person acquires control over psychic energy, the basic fuel upon which all thinking depends.

In everyday life, it is rare for the different contents of experience to be in synchrony with each other. At work my attention might be focused, because the boss gave me a job to do that requires intense thinking. But this particular job is not one I ordinarily would want to do, so I am not very motivated intrinsically. At the same time, I am distracted by feelings of anxiety about my teenage son's erratic behavior. So while part of my mind is concentrated on the task, I am not completely involved in it. It is not that my mind is in total chaos, but there is quite a bit of entropy in my consciousness—thoughts, emotions, and intentions come into focus and then disappear, producing contrary impulses, and pulling my attention in different directions. Or, to consider another example, I may enjoy a drink with friends after work, but I feel guilty about not going home to the family and mad at myself for wasting time and money.

Neither of these scenarios is particularly unusual. Everyday life is full of them: rarely do we feel the serenity that comes when heart, will, and mind are on the same page. Conflicting desires, intentions, and thoughts jostle each other in consciousness, and we are helpless to keep them in line.

But now let us consider some alternatives. Imagine, for instance, that you are skiing down a slope and your full attention is focused on the movements of the body, the position of the skis, the air whistling past your face, and the snow-shrouded trees running by. There is no room in your awareness for conflicts or contradictions; you know that a distracting thought or emotion might get you buried facedown in the snow. And who wants to get distracted? The run is so perfect that all you want is for it to last forever, to immerse yourself completely in the experience.

If skiing does not mean much to you, substitute your favorite activity for this vignette. It could be singing in a choir, programming a computer, dancing, playing bridge, reading a good book. Or if you love your job, as many people do, it could be when you are getting immersed in a complicated surgical operation or a close business deal. Or this complete immersion in the activity may occur in a social interaction, as when good friends talk with each other, or when a mother plays with her baby. What is common to such moments is that consciousness is full of experiences, and these experiences are in harmony with each other. Contrary to what happens all too often in everyday life, in moments such as these what we feel, what we wish, and what we think are in harmony.

These exceptional moments are what I have called *flow experiences*. The metaphor of "flow" is one that many people have used to describe the sense of effortless action they feel in moments that stand out as the best in their lives. Athletes refer to it as "being in the zone," religious mystics as being in "ecstasy," artists and musicians as aesthetic rapture. Athletes, mystics, and artists do very different things when they reach flow, yet their descriptions of the experience are remarkably similar.

Flow tends to occur when a person faces a clear set of goals that require appropriate responses. It is easy to enter flow in games such as chess, tennis, or poker, because they have goals and rules for action that make it possible for the player to act without questioning what should be done, and how. For the duration of the game the player lives in a self-contained universe where everything is black and white. The

same clarity of goals is present if you perform a religious ritual, play a musical piece, weave a rug, write a computer program, climb a mountain, or perform surgery. Activities that
induce flow could be called "flow activities" because they
make it more likely for the experience to occur. In contrast
to normal life, flow activities allow a person to focus on goals
that are clear and compatible.

Another characteristic of flow activities is that they provide immediate feedback. They make it clear how well you
are doing. After each move of a game you can tell whether
you have improved your position or not. With each step, the
climber knows that he has inched higher. After each bar of a
song you can hear whether the notes you sang matched the
score. The weaver can see whether the last row of stitches fits
the pattern of the tapestry as it should. The surgeon can see
as she cuts whether the knife has avoided cutting any arteries,
or whether there is sudden bleeding. On the job or at home
we might go for long periods without a clue as to how we
stand, while in flow we can usually tell.

Flow tends to occur when a person's skills are fully involved in overcoming a challenge that is just about manageable. Optimal experiences usually involve a fine balance
between one's ability to act, and the available opportunities
for action (see figure 1). If challenges are too high one gets
frustrated, then worried, and eventually anxious. If challenges are too low relative to one's skills one gets relaxed,
then bored. If both challenges and skills are perceived to be
low, one gets to feel apathetic. But when high challenges are
matched with high skills, then the deep involvement that sets
flow apart from ordinary life is likely to occur. The climber
will feel it when the mountain demands all his strength, the
singer when the song demands the full range of her vocal
ability, the weaver when the design of the tapestry is more
complex than anything attempted before, and the surgeon
when the operation involves new procedures or requires an
unexpected variation. A typical day is full of anxiety and

Figure 1
The quality of experience as a function of the relationship between challenges and skills. Optimal experience, or flow, occurs when both variables are high.

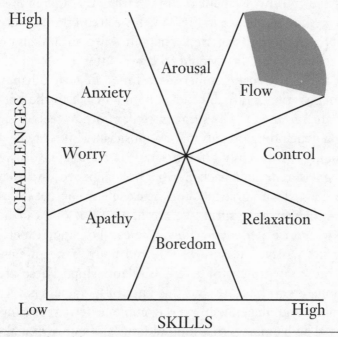

Sources: Adapted from Massimini & Carli 1988; Csikszentmihalyi 1990.

boredom. Flow experiences provide the flashes of intense living against this dull background.

When goals are clear, feedback relevant, and challenges and skills are in balance, attention becomes ordered and fully invested. Because of the total demand on psychic energy, a person in flow is completely focused. There is no space in consciousness for distracting thoughts, irrelevant feelings. Self-consciousness disappears, yet one feels stronger than usual. The sense of time is distorted: hours seem to pass by in minutes. When a person's entire being is stretched in the full functioning of body and mind, whatever one does becomes worth doing for its own sake; living becomes its own justification. In the harmonious focusing of physical and psychic energy, life finally comes into its own.

It is the full involvement of flow, rather than happiness, that makes for excellence in life. When we are in flow, we are not happy, because to experience happiness we must focus on our inner states, and that would take away attention from the task at hand. If a rock climber takes time out to feel happy while negotiating a difficult move, he might fall to the bottom of the mountain. The surgeon can't afford to feel happy during a demanding operation, or a musician while playing a challenging score. Only after the task is completed do we have the leisure to look back on what has happened, and then we are flooded with gratitude for the excellence of that experience—then, in retrospect, we are happy. But one can be happy without experiencing flow. We can be happy experiencing the passive pleasure of a rested body, a warm sunshine, the contentment of a serene relationship. These are also moments to treasure, but this kind of happiness is very vulnerable and dependent on favorable external circumstances. The happiness that follows flow is of our own making, and it leads to increasing complexity and growth in consciousness.

The graph in figure 1 can also be read to indicate why flow leads to personal growth. Suppose a person is in the area marked "Arousal" on the graph. This is not a bad condition to be in; in arousal a person feels mentally focused, active, and involved—but not very strong, cheerful, or in control. How can one return to the more enjoyable flow state? The answer is obvious: by learning new skills. Or let us look at the area labeled "Control." This is also a positive state of experience, where one feels happy, strong, satisfied. But one tends to lack concentration, involvement, and a feeling that what one does is important. So how does one get back to flow? By increasing challenges. Thus arousal and control are very important states for learning. The other conditions are less favorable. When a person is anxious or worried, for example, the step to flow often seems too far, and one retreats to a less challenging situation instead of trying to cope.

Thus the flow experience acts as a magnet for learning—that is, for developing new levels of challenges and skills. In an ideal situation, a person would be constantly growing while enjoying whatever he or she did. Alas, we know this is not the case. Usually we feel too bored and apathetic to move into the flow zone, so we prefer to fill our mind with ready-made, prepackaged stimulation off the video shelf or some other kind of professional entertainment. Or we feel too overwhelmed to imagine we could develop the appropriate skills, so we prefer to descend into the apathy engendered by artificial relaxants like drugs or alcohol. It takes energy to achieve optimal experiences, and all too often we are unable, or unwilling, to put out the initial effort.

How often do people experience flow? That depends on whether we are willing to count even mild approximations of the ideal condition as instances of flow. For example, if one asks a sample of typical Americans: "Do you ever get involved in something so deeply that nothing else seems to matter, and you lose track of time?" roughly one in five will say that yes, this happens to them often, as much as several times a day; whereas about 15 percent will say that no, this never happens to them. These frequencies seem to be quite stable and universal. For instance, in a recent survey of a representative sample of 6,469 Germans the same question was answered in the following way: Often, 23 percent; Sometimes, 40 percent; Rarely, 25 percent; Never or Don't Know, 12 percent. Of course if one were to count only the most intense and exalted flow experiences, then their frequency would be much more rare.

Flow is generally reported when a person is doing his or her favorite activity—gardening, listening to music, bowling, cooking a good meal. It also occurs when driving, when talk-

ing to friends, and surprisingly often at work. Very rarely do people report flow in passive leisure activities, such as watching television or relaxing. But because almost any activity can produce flow provided the relevant elements are present, it is possible to improve the quality of life by making sure that clear goals, immediate feedback, skills balanced to action opportunities, and the remaining conditions of flow are as much as possible a constant part of everyday life.

THREE

How We Feel When Doing Different Things

The quality of life depends on what we do in the seventy or so years we are allotted, and on what passes in consciousness during that time. Different activities typically affect the quality of experience in rather predictable ways. If all through life we only do depressing things, it is unlikely that we will end up having lived a very happy life. Usually each activity has both positive and negative qualities. When we eat, for instance, we tend to feel more positive affect than usual; a graph of a person's level of happiness during the day resembles the profile of the Golden Gate Bridge across San Francisco Bay, with the high points corresponding to meal-times. At the same time, mental concentration tends to be rather low when a person eats, and one rarely experiences flow.

The psychological effects of activities are not linear, but depend on their systemic relation to everything else we do.

35

For instance, even though food is a source of good moods, we cannot achieve happiness by eating around the clock. Meals raise the level of happiness, but only when we spend around 5 percent of our waking time eating; if we spent 100 percent of the day eating, food would quickly cease to be rewarding. The same is true of most of the other good things in life: sex, relaxation, television watching, in small doses, tend to improve the quality of daily life considerably, but the effects are not additive; a point of diminishing returns is quickly reached.

A very condensed view of how people typically experience the various components of their daily life is presented in table 2. As we see, when adults work (or when children do schoolwork) they tend to be less happy than average and their motivation is considerably below normal. At the same time their level of concentration is relatively quite high, so their mental processes seem to be engaged more than they are the rest of the day. Surprisingly, work also often produces flow, presumably because challenges and skills tend to be high when working, and goals and feedback are often clear and immediate.

Of course "work" is such a broad category that it seems impossible to make an accurate generalization about it. In the first place, it makes sense to think that the quality of experience when working would depend on the kind of job one has. A traffic controller must concentrate much more on his job than a night watchman. A self-employed entrepreneur presumably is much more motivated to work than a clerk in a government office. While this is true, the characteristic signature of work persists despite the very real differences. For example, the experience of managers when they are on the job resembles that of assembly-line workers much more than it resembles their own experience when they are at home.

Another problem of generalizing about work is that the same job will have many aspects that are experienced differ-

Table 2

The Quality of Experience in Everyday Activities

Based on daytime activities reported by representative adults and teenagers in recent U.S. studies.

The typical quality of experience in various activities is indicated as follows:

— negative; —— very negative; o average or neutral; + positive; ++ very positive

	Happiness	Motivation	Concentration	Flow
Productive Activities				
Working at work or studying	-	——	++	+
Maintenance Activities				
Housework	-	-	o	-
Eating	++	++	-	o
Grooming	o	o	o	o
Driving, transportation	o	o	+	+
Leisure Activities				
Media (TV and reading)	o	++	-	-
Hobbies, sports, movies	+	++	+	++
Talking, socializing, sex	++	++	o	+
Idling, resting	o	+	-	——

Sources: Csikszentmihalyi and Csikszentmihalyi 1988; Csikszentmihalyi and Graef 1980; Csikszentmihalyi and LeFevre 1989; Csikszentmihalyi, Rathunde, and Whalen 1993; Kubey and Csikszentmihalyi 1990; and Larson and Richards 1994.

ently. A manager might love to work on a project but hate to sit in conferences, while an assembler might love to set up a machine but hate to take inventory. Nevertheless, it is still possible to talk about the distinctive quality of the work experience in comparison with other general activity categories. The more it resembles a flow activity, the more involved we become, and the more positive the experience. When the job presents clear goals, unambiguous feedback, a sense of control, challenges that match the worker's skills, and few distractions, the feelings it provides are not that different from what one experiences in a sport or an artistic performance.

Maintenance activities are quite varied in terms of their experiential profile. Few people enjoy housework, which tends to be generally negative or neutral along all dimensions. If one were to look in finer detail, however, it would turn out that cooking is often a positive experience, especially compared to cleaning the house. Personal care—washing, dressing, and so forth—is usually neither positive nor negative. Eating, as mentioned earlier, is one of the most positive parts of the day in terms of affect and motivation, whereas it is low in cognitive activity and seldom an occasion of flow.

Driving a car, which is the last major component of the maintenance category, is a surprisingly positive part of life. While neutral in terms of happiness and motivation, it requires skill and concentration, and some people experience flow more often while driving than in any other part of their lives.

As one would expect, leisure tends to include the more positive experiences of the day. Leisure is when people feel the most motivated, when they say that they want to do whatever they are doing. Yet here too, we find some surprises. Passive leisure, which includes media consumption and resting, while it is a motivating and reasonably happy activity, involves little mental focus, and rarely produces flow. Socializing—talking

with people without much ulterior purpose except the interaction itself—is generally highly positive even though it seldom involves high mental concentration. Romance and sex
provide some of the best moments of the day, but for most
people these activities are rather rare, so they fail to make
much of a difference in the overall quality of life unless they
are embedded in a context of an enduring relationship that
provides emotional and intellectual rewards as well.

Active leisure is another source of extremely positive experiences. When people do a hobby, get involved in exercise,
play a musical instrument, or go out to a movie or restaurant,
they tend to be more happy, motivated, concentrated, and
more often in flow than in any other part of the day. It is in
these contexts that all the various dimensions of experience
are most intensely focused and in harmony with each other.
It is important to remember, however, that active leisure
usually takes up only between a fourth and a fifth of a person's free time, and for many it is vastly overshadowed by the
amount of time spent in passive leisure activities such as
watching television.

Another way to look at the pattern in table 2 is to ask,
Which activities are happiest? Which are most motivated? If
we do that, we see that happiness is highest when eating,
when in active leisure, and when talking with people; it is
lowest when working on the job or around the house. Motivation follows a similar pattern, with the addition that passive leisure, which does not make one happy, is something
we usually want to do anyway. Concentration is highest on
the job, when driving, and in active leisure—these are the activities that during the day require the most mental effort.
The same activities also provide the highest rates of flow,
and so does socializing with others. When we look at the pattern this way, it again shows that active leisure provides the
best experience overall, while housework, personal care, and
idling provide the worst.

So the first step in improving the quality of life consists in

engineering daily activities so that one gets the most rewarding experiences from them. This sounds simple, but the inertia of habit and social pressure are so strong that many
people have no idea which components of their lives they actually enjoy, and which contribute to stress and depression.
Keeping a diary or reflecting on the past day in the evening
are ways to take stock systematically of the various influences
on one's moods. After it is clear which activities produce the
high points in one's day, it becomes possible to start experimenting—by increasing the frequency of the positive ones,
and decreasing that of the others.

A somewhat extreme example of how this might work was
reported by Marten DeVries, a psychiatrist in charge of a
large community mental health center in the Netherlands. In
his hospital, patients are routinely given the ESM to find out
what they do all day, what they think about, and how they
feel. One of the patients, a chronic schizophrenic woman
who had been hospitalized for over ten years, showed the
usual confused thought patterns and low affect of severe
mental pathology. But during the two weeks of the ESM
study, she reported quite positive moods twice. In both cases
she had been taking care of her fingernails. Thinking that it
was worth a try, the staff had a professional manicurist teach
her the skills of her trade. The patient took eagerly to the in-
struction, and she was soon caring for the nails of the rest of
the patients. Her disposition changed so drastically that she
was released into the community under supervision; she
hung a shingle on her door, and within the year she was self-
sufficient. No one knows why paring nails was the challenge
this woman needed, and if one interpreted this story psycho-
analytically, perhaps no one would want to know. The fact is
that for this one person at this stage in life, being a manicurist allowed at least a pale semblance of flow to enter her
life.

Professor Fausto Massimini and his staff at the University
of Milan, Italy, have also adapted the ESM as a diagnostic

tool, and use it to tailor-make interventions that by changing the pattern of activities may improve well-being. If a patient is always alone, they find work or volunteer activities that will bring him in social contact. If she is terrified of people, they take her for walks in the crowded streets of the city, or to spectacles and dances. The comforting presence of the therapist in the problematic situation, as opposed to the safe office, often helps to remove the obstacles to the patients' involvement with activities that improve the quality of their lives.

Creative people are especially good at ordering their lives so that what they do, when, and with whom will enable them to do their best work. If what they need is spontaneity and disorder, then they make sure to have that, too. The novelist Richard Stern's description of the "rhythms" of his daily life is quite typical:

> My guess is that it resembles other people's rhythms. Anybody who does work either has a routine or imposes on his life certain periods in which he can be alone or in which he collaborates. At any rate, he works out a sort of schedule for himself and this is not simply an external, exoskeletal phenomenon. It seems to me it has much to do with the relationship of your own physiological, hormonal, organic self and its relationship to the world outside. Components can be so ordinary as: do you read the newspaper in the morning. I used to do that years ago, and I stopped for years and years, which altered the rhythm of my day, and so on. One drinks a glass of wine in the evenings at certain times, when the blood sugar's low, and one looks forward to it. And then of course those hours in which one works.

A major feature of daily rhythms is going in and out of solitude. Over and over, our findings suggest that people get depressed when they are alone, and they revive when they rejoin the company of others. Alone a person generally reports low happiness, aversive motivation, low concentration, apathy, and an entire string of other negative states such as passivity, loneliness, detachment, and low self-esteem. Being alone affects most those individuals who have the fewest resources: those who have been unable to get an education, who are poor, single, or divorced. Pathological states are often invisible as long as the person is with others; they take effect mostly when we are alone. The moods that people diagnosed with chronic depression or with eating disorders experience are indistinguishable from those of healthy people—as long as they are in company and doing something that requires concentration. But when they are alone with nothing to do, their minds begin to be occupied by depressing thoughts, and their consciousness becomes entropic. This is also true, to a less pronounced extent, of everyone else.

The reason is that when we have to interact with another person, even a stranger, our attention becomes structured by external demands. The presence of the other imposes goals and provides feedback. Even the simplest interaction—like that of asking another person the correct time—has its own challenges, which we confront with our interpersonal skills. Our tone of voice, a smile, our bearing and demeanor are part of the skills we need in stopping a stranger on the street, and making a good impression. In more intimate encounters, the level of both challenges and skills can grow very high. Thus interactions have many of the characteristics of flow activities, and they certainly require the orderly investment of psychic energy. By contrast, when we are alone with nothing to do there is no reason to concentrate, and what happens then is that the mind begins to unravel, and soon finds something to worry about.

Being with friends provides the most positive experiences. Here people report being happy, alert, sociable, cheerful, motivated. This is especially true of teenagers, but it also holds for retired seniors in their seventies and eighties. The importance of friendships on well-being is difficult to overestimate. The quality of life improves immensely when there is at least one other person who is willing to listen to our troubles, and to support us emotionally. National surveys find that when someone claims to have five or more friends with whom they can discuss important problems, they are 60 percent more likely to say that they are "very happy."

Experience while with the family tends to be average, not as good as with friends, not as bad as when alone. But this average is also the result of wide swings; one can get extremely aggravated at home one moment and be thoroughly ecstatic the next. On the job, adults tend to have greater concentration and cognitive involvement, but they are more motivated when at home, and are happier there. The same holds true for children in school compared to home. Family members often experience their interactions differently from each other. For instance, when fathers are with their children, they typically report positive moods. So do their children up to grade 5. Afterwards, children report increasingly negative moods when with their fathers (at least until grade 8, after which there are no data available).

The strong effects of companionship on the quality of experience suggest that investing psychic energy in relationships is a good way to improve life. Even the passive, superficial conversations at a neighborhood bar can stave off depression. But for real growth, it is necessary to find people whose opinions are interesting and whose conversation is stimulating. A more difficult, but in the long run even more useful, skill to acquire is the ability to tolerate solitude, and to even enjoy it.

Everyday life unfolds in various locations—the home, the car, the office, streets, and restaurants. In addition to activities and companionships, locations also have an effect on the quality of experience. Teenagers, for instance, feel best when they are furthest away from adult supervision, such as in a public park. They feel most constrained in school, in churches, and other places where their behavior must conform to others' expectations. Adults also prefer public places, where they are likely to be with their friends and involved in voluntary leisure activities. This is especially true for women, for whom being out of the house often means a relief from drudgery, whereas for men being in public is more often related to work and other responsibilities.

For many people, driving a car gives the most consistent sense of freedom and control; they call it their "thinking machine" because while driving they can concentrate on their problems without interruptions, and resolve emotional conflicts in the protective cocoon of their personal vehicle. One Chicago steelworker, whenever his personal problems become too stressful, jumps into his car after work, and drives west until he reaches the Mississippi River. He spends a few hours at a picnic site on the banks, watching the silent waters drift by. Then he returns to the car, and by the time he gets home, with the dawn rising over Lake Michigan, he feels at peace. For many families, the car has also become the location for togetherness. At home parents and children are often dispersed in different rooms, doing different things; when on an outing in the car, they talk, sing, or play games together.

Different rooms of the house also have their peculiar emotional profile, in large part because each is the setting for a different kind of activity. For instance, men report good moods when they are in the basement, whereas women do not; probably because men go to the basement to relax or work on hobbies, whereas their wives are more likely to go there to do the laundry. Women report some of their best moods in the house when they are in the bathroom, where they are relatively free from the demands of the family, and in the kitchen, where they are in control and involved in cooking, which is an activity that is relatively pleasant. (Men actually enjoy cooking much more than women, no doubt because they do it less than one-tenth as often, and thus can choose to do it when they feel like it.)

Although much has been written about how the environment in which one lives affects one's mind, there is actually very little systematic knowledge on this topic. Since time immemorial, artists, scholars, and religious mystics have chosen carefully the surroundings that best allowed serenity and inspiration. Buddhist monks settled down at the sources of the Ganges River, Chinese scholars wrote in pavilions on picturesque islands, Christian monasteries were built on the hills with the best views. In contemporary America, research institutes and corporate R&D laboratories are generally sited among rolling hills, with ducks in the reflecting ponds or the ocean across the horizon.

If we are to trust the reports of creative thinkers and artists, congenial surroundings are often the source of inspiration and creativity. They often echo Franz Liszt's words, which he wrote on romantic Lake Como: "I feel that the various features of Nature around me . . . provoke an emotional reaction in the depth of my soul, which I have tried to transcribe in music." Manfred Eigen, who won the Nobel Prize in chemistry in 1967, says that some of his most important insights came from winter trips to the Swiss Alps, where he invited colleagues from all over the world to ski and talk about science. If one reads the biographies of physicists like Bohr, Heisenberg, Chandrashekhar, and Bethe, one gets the impression that without hikes in the mountains and the vision of night skies their science would not have amounted to much.

To make a creative change in the quality of experience, it might be useful to experiment with one's surroundings as well as with activities and companions. Outings and vacations help to clear the mind, to change perspectives, to look at one's situation with a fresh eye. Taking charge of one's home or office environment—throwing out the excess, redecorating to one's taste, making it personal and psychologically comfortable, could be the first step in reordering one's life.

We often hear of how important biorhythms are, and how differently we feel on Blue Mondays as compared to weekends. In fact, the way each day is experienced changes considerably from morning to night. Early mornings and late nights are low on many of the positive emotions, mealtimes and afternoons are high. The largest changes occur when children leave school and when adults come home from work. Not all the contents of consciousness travel in the same direction: when out with friends in the evening teenagers report increasing excitement hour after hour, but at the same time they also feel that they are gradually losing control. In addition to these general trends, there are a number of individual differences: morning persons and night persons relate to time of day in opposite ways.

Despite the bad reputation of certain days of the week, on the whole people seem to experience each day more or less like the next. True, as one would expect, Friday afternoons and Saturdays are marginally better than Sunday evenings and Monday mornings, but the differences are less than one would expect. Much depends on how we plan our time: Sunday mornings can be quite depressing if one has nothing to do, but if we look forward to a scheduled activity or a familiar ritual such as going to a church service, then it can be a high point of the week.

One interesting finding is that people report significantly more physical symptoms, such as headaches and backaches, on weekends and at times when they are not studying or working. Even the pain of women with cancer is tolerable when they are with friends, or involved in an activity; it flares up when they are alone with nothing to do. Apparently when psychic energy is not committed to a definite task it is easier to notice what goes wrong in our bodies. This fits with what we know about the flow experience: when playing a close tournament, chess players can go for hours without noticing hunger or headache; athletes in a competition can ignore pain and fatigue until the event is over. When attention is focused, minor aches and pains have no chance to register in consciousness.

Again, with time of day as with the other parameters of life, it is important to find out what rhythms are most congenial to you personally. There is no day or hour that is best for everyone. Reflection helps to identify one's preferences, and experimentation with different alternatives—getting up earlier, taking a nap in the afternoon, eating at different times—helps to find the best set of options.

In all of these examples, we proceeded as if persons were passive objects whose internal states are affected by what they do, who they are with, where they are, and so forth. While this is true in part, in the last analysis it is not the external conditions that count, but what we make of them. It is perfectly possible to be happy doing housework with nobody around, to be motivated when working, to concentrate when talking to a child. In other words, the excellence of daily life finally depends not on what we do, but on *how* we do it.

Nevertheless, before looking at how one can control the quality of experience directly by transforming information in consciousness, it is important to reflect on the effects that the daily environment—the places, people, activities, and times of day—has on us. Even the most accomplished mystic, detached from all influences, will prefer to sit under one particular tree, eat a certain food, and be with one companion rather than another. Most of us are much more responsive to the situations in which we find ourselves.

Thus the first step in improving the quality of life is to pay close attention to what we do every day, and to notice how we feel in different activities, places, times of day, and with different companions. Although the general trends will probably apply also in your case—you'll find yourself happier at mealtimes and most often in flow when in active leisure—

there might be also surprising revelations. It may turn out that you really like being alone. Or that you like working more than you thought. Or that reading makes you feel better afterwards than watching television. Or vice versa on all these counts. There is no law that says we have to experience life in the same way. What is vital is to find out what works out best in your case.

≡FOUR

The Paradox of Work

Work generally takes up a third of the time available for living. Work is a strange experience: it provides some of the most intense and satisfying moments, it gives a sense of pride and identity, yet it is something most of us are glad to avoid. On the one hand, recent surveys report that 84 percent of American men and 77 percent of women say they would continue to work even if they inherited enough money so they no longer needed a job. On the other hand, according to several ESM studies, when people are signaled at work they endorse the item "I wish I was doing something else" more than at any other time of the day. Another example of this contradictory attitude is a book in which two eminent German social scientists, using the same survey results, developed opposite arguments. One claimed, among other things, that German workers disliked work, and those who disliked it more were happier overall. The second responded that workers only dislike work because they are brainwashed by the media on ideological grounds, and those who like their work lead richer lives. The point is that there was reasonable evidence for both conclusions.

Because work is so important in terms of the amount of time it takes and the intensity of effects it produces in consciousness, it is essential to face up to its ambiguities if one wishes to improve the quality of life. A first step in that direction is to briefly review how work activities evolved in history, and the contradictory values that were attributed to it, which still now affect our attitudes and experiences.

Work as we know it now is a very recent historical development. It didn't exist before the great agricultural revolutions that made intensive farming possible about twelve thousand years ago. During the previous millions of years of human evolution, each man and woman provided for self and kin. But there was no such thing as working *for* someone else; for hunter-gatherers work was seamlessly integrated with the rest of life.

In the classical Western civilizations of Greece and Rome, philosophers reflected the public opinion about work, which was that it should be avoided at all costs. Idleness was considered a virtue. According to Aristotle, only a man who did not have to work could be happy. Roman philosophers agreed that "wage labor is sordid and unworthy of a free man . . . craft labor is sordid, and so is the business of retailing." The ideal was to conquer or buy productive land, and then hire a staff of stewards to supervise its cultivation by slaves or indentured serfs. In Imperial Rome, about 20 percent of the male adult population did not have to work. By having attained a life of idleness, they believed that they had reached excellence in their lives. In Republican times, there was some substance to this belief: members of the ruling class volunteered their time to fill military and administrative duties that helped the community and gave room for personal potential to expand. But after centuries of ease, the idle classes withdrew from public life and used their free time to consume luxury and entertainment instead.

Work, for the majority of people, started to change radically in Europe about five hundred years ago. It took another quantum jump two hundred years ago, and still continues to change at a rapid rate right now. Until the thirteenth century, almost all energy for work depended on human or animal muscle. Only a few primitive engines, such as water-mills, helped to alleviate the burden. Then slowly windmills with a variety of gears began to take over the chore of grinding grains, hauling water, blasting furnaces where metals were forged. The development of steam engines, and later electricity, further revolutionized the way we transform energy and make a living.

An offshoot of these technological breakthroughs has been that work, instead of being seen as simply a physical effort that an ox or a horse could do better, began to be seen as a skilled activity, a manifestation of human ingenuity and creativity. By Calvin's time, it made sense to take the "work ethic" seriously. And it is for this reason also that Karl Marx could later reverse the classical evaluation of labor, and claim that only through productive activity can we realize our human potential. His position did not contradict the spirit of Aristotle's opposite claim, that only leisure made men free. It is just that, by the nineteenth century, work seemed to offer more creative options than idleness did.

During the decades of affluence following World War II, most jobs in America might have been boring and bland, but on the whole they provided decent conditions and reasonable security. There was much talk about a new era in which work would be abolished, or at least transformed into purely white-collar supervisory tasks that would take only a few hours a week to accomplish. It didn't take long to see how utopian these forecasts had been. The global competition that allowed the underpaid populations of Asia and South America to compete in the labor market is again giving work in the United States a grim reputation. Increasingly, as the social safety net is in danger of unraveling, people have to work more often in arbitrary conditions and without much security about the future. So even now, at the close of the twentieth century, the deep ambiguity of work still haunts us. We know it is one of the most important elements of our lives, yet while we do it we would rather not be doing it.

How do we learn these conflicting attitudes toward work? And how do young people these days learn the skills and discipline required to do adult productive work? These questions are by no means trivial. With each generation, work becomes an increasingly fuzzy concept, and it becomes harder for young people to know what jobs will be waiting for them when they grow up, and to learn how to prepare for them.

In the past, and to a certain extent even now, in hunting or fishing societies in Alaska or Melanesia, we can still see what the pattern used to be everywhere else in the world: children from an early age participated in their parents' work, and gradually found themselves performing as productive adults without missing a beat along the way. An Inuit boy was given a toy bow at age two, and he started practicing shooting right away. By four he might be expected to shoot a ptarmigan, at six a rabbit, and from there he graduated to caribou and seal. His sister went through a similar progression helping the women of her kin group to cure hides, cook, sew, and care for younger siblings. There was no question about what one should do when one grew up—there were no options to choose from, there was only a single path to productive adulthood.

When the agricultural revolution made cities possible about ten thousand years ago, specialized jobs started to appear, and a degree of choice opened up for young people. Still, most of them ended up doing what their parents did, which until a few centuries ago was mainly farming. It was not until the sixteenth and seventeenth centuries that a large number of young people began to move from farms to cities, to try their luck in the burgeoning urban economy. According to some estimates, by age twelve as many as 80 percent of country girls in some parts of Europe left their farmer parents, whereas boys left on the average two years later. Most of the jobs waiting in London or Paris were in what now would be called the service industries, as charwomen, coachmen, porters, or laundresses.

The situation is very different now. In a recent study, we asked a few thousand representative American teenagers what jobs they expected to have when they grew up. The results are presented in table 3. What it shows is that adolescents have unrealistically high expectations of becoming professionals: 15 percent of them expect to become either doctors or lawyers, which is almost fifteen times higher than the actual proportion of doctors and lawyers in the labor force according to the 1990 Census. Most of the 244 adolescents who expect to become professional athletes will also be disappointed, since they overestimate their chances by about 500-fold. Minority children from the inner city look forward to professional careers at the same rate as affluent suburban children, despite the fact that the unemployment rate for young African-Americans in some cities has been near 50 percent.

The lack of realism about future career options is in part due to the rapidly changing nature of adult jobs, but it is also caused by many young people's isolation from meaningful job opportunities and adult working models. Contrary to what one might expect, affluent teenagers actually work more often in high school than poorer students, even though they don't have to. And exposure to productive tasks in the home, the neighborhood, and the community is much greater for children who grow up in wealthy and stable environments. There one can actually find fifteen year olds who plan to become architects and who have learned to draft in a realtive's architectural firm, who have helped design an extension to a neighbor's house, who have interned with a local construction company—although overall such opportunities are infrequent. In an inner city high school, the most popular informal career counselor was a school guard who helped sharp young boys find jobs with the gangs, and directed good-looking girls toward so-called modeling jobs.

According to the ESM results, it seems that young people learn their elders' ambivalence toward work quite early. By age ten or eleven, they have internalized the pattern that is typical of society at large. When they are asked to say whether what they are doing is more like "work" or more like "play" (or like "both" or "neither") sixth graders almost invariably say that academic classes in school are work, and doing sports is play. The interesting thing is that whenever adolescents are doing something they label as work, they typically say that what they do is important for their future,

Table 3
What Jobs Do American Teenagers Expect to Have?

The ten most frequently expected future jobs, based on interviews with a sample of 3,891 U.S. adolescents

Occupation	Rank	% of sample
Doctor	1	10
Business Person	2	7
Lawyer	3	7
Teacher	4	7
Athlete	5	6
Engineer	6	5
Nurse	7	4
Accountant, CPA	8	3
Psychologist	9	3
Architect	10	3
Other	-	45

Source: Adapted from Bidwell, Csikszentmihalyi, Hedges, and Schneider 1997, in press.

requires high concentration, and induces high self-esteem. Yet they are also less happy and motivated than average when what they do is like work. On the other hand, when they are doing something they label as play, they see it as having low importance and requiring little concentration, but they are happy and motivated. In other words, the split between work that is necessary but unpleasant, and pleasant but useless play, is well established by late childhood. It does get even more pronounced as adolescents go through high school.

When the same adolescents eventually start working, they report exactly the same pattern of experience from their workplace. In the U.S., almost nine out of ten teenagers are employed sometime during high school, a much higher proportion than in other technologically advanced countries like Germany or Japan, where there are fewer opportunities for part-time work—and where parents prefer their children to spend as much time as possible studying, rather than being distracted by jobs irrelevant to their future careers. In our study, 57 percent of tenth graders and 86 percent of twelfth graders have held paying jobs, usually serving fast food, as clerks or salespersons, or as baby-sitters. When teenagers are paged on their jobs, they report very elevated self-esteem. They see what they do as important and requiring great concentration. But they are less happy than usual (although not as unhappy as in school), and they don't enjoy themselves. In other words, the pattern of ambivalence is set by the very first steps of their working lives.

But work is definitely not the worst thing adolescents experience. The worst condition they report is when what they do is neither like work nor like play. When this is the case—usually in maintenance activities, passive leisure, or socializing—their self-esteem is lowest, what they do has no importance, and their happiness and motivation are also below average. Yet for adolescents "neither work nor play" takes up on the average 35 percent of the day. Some, especially children whose parents have little education, feel that half or more of what they do is of this kind. A person who grows up experiencing most of the day as neither important nor enjoyable is unlikely to find much meaning in the future.

The attitudes set in the early years continue to color how we experience work during the rest of our lives. On the job, people tend to use their mind and body to its fullest, and consequently feel that what they do is important, and feel good about themselves while doing it. Yet their motivation is worse than when they are at home, and so is the quality of their moods. Despite huge differences in salary, prestige, and freedom, managers tend to feel only somewhat more creative and active on the job, while clerical and assembly-line workers are no more unhappy and dissatisfied.

Men and women, however, tend to experience work outside the home in different ways. Traditionally, men's identity and self-respect have been based on the ability to obtain energy from the environment for their own and their families' use. Whether the satisfaction a man gets from doing a necessary job is partly genetically programmed, or is entirely learned from the culture, the fact is that more or less everywhere a man who is not a provider is to some extent a misfit. Women's self-esteem, on the other hand, has traditionally been based on their ability to create a physical and emotional environment suitable for the rearing of children and the comfort of grown-ups. No matter how enlightened we have become in terms of trying to avoid these gender stereotypes, they are far from gone. Teenage boys still wish to become police officers, firefighters, and engineers, while girls look forward to becoming homemakers, nurses, and teachers—although girls nowadays also expect to become professionals, such as doctors and lawyers, at a rate that is even higher than for boys.

Because of the different role of paid work in the psychic economy of men and women, the response of the two genders to their jobs is generally different. Leaving aside those still relatively few career women whose primary identification is with their jobs, most women who work at clerical, service, and even managerial occupations tend to think of their outside job as something they want to do rather than something they have to do. Work is more voluntary for many women; it is more like play, something that they could take or leave. Many of them feel that whatever happens on the job is not that important—and thus, paradoxically, they can enjoy it more. Even if things go wrong and they are laid off it will not hurt their self-esteem. As opposed to men, their self-image depends more heavily on what happens to their families. Having a destitute parent or a child who has trouble in school is a much greater load on their minds than whatever can happen at work.

As a result, and especially in comparison with the work they have to do around the house, women generally experience employment more positively than men. For instance, in an ESM study conducted with couples where both partners worked, Reed Larson found that women reported relatively more positive emotions than men when doing clerical work, computer work, sales, meetings, working on the phone, reading work-related material, and so on. The only job-related activity women experienced less positively than men was when they worked at home on projects brought back from the office, no doubt because in those situations they felt responsible also for the household tasks in addition to those related to the job.

The double jeopardy a family and a career imposes can be a heavy burden on the self-esteem of women. In a study of mothers of small children who worked either full time, part time, or only a few hours a week, Anne Wells found that the highest levels of self-esteem were reported by women who worked least, and the lowest by those who worked most—this despite the fact that all women enjoyed working outside for pay more than they enjoyed working at home. Again this finding suggests the ambiguous meaning of self-esteem. Full-time, professional women with families might have lower self-esteem not because they are accomplishing less, but because they expect more from themselves than they can possibly deliver.

These issues bring into focus how arbitrary the division is between work done for pay, and the housework women have been traditionally expected to do for their families. As Elise Boulding and other social economists have pointed out, maintenance work might not be productive, but if it had to be paid for as a service, the bill would run close to the GNP. The cost of mothers' nurturance of children, care of the sick, cooking, cleaning, and so forth at the market rate would double the national payroll, and perhaps force us to adopt a more humane economy. In the meantime, however, while doing housework may bolster a married woman's self-esteem, it does not contribute much to her emotional well-being. Cooking, shopping, driving the family around, and caring for children are accompanied by only average emotions. But cleaning the house, cleaning the kitchen, doing laundry, fixing things around the house, and balancing the checkbook are generally among the most negative experiences in a woman's day.

Work has severe drawbacks, but its lack is worse. The ancient philosophers had much good to say in favor of idleness, but what they had in mind was the idleness of a landowner with many serfs and slaves. When idleness is forced on someone without a handsome income, it just produces a severe drop in self-esteem, and general listlessness. As John Hayworth, a psychologist at the University of Manchester, has shown, young men out of work, even when paid relatively generous unemployment compensation, have a very hard time finding satisfaction in their lives. In a compilation of studies involving 170,000 workers in sixteen nations, Ronald Ingelhart found that 83 percent of white-collar workers, 77 percent of manual workers, but only 61 percent of the unemployed said that they were satisfied with their lives. The Bible's suggestion that man was made to enjoy the bounty of creation without having to work for it does not seem to jibe with the facts. Without the goal and the challenges usually provided by a job, only a rare self-discipline can keep the mind focused intensely enough to insure a meaningful life.

The finding through our ESM studies that if one looks at the sources of flow in the lives of adults, one finds more occasions of it on the job than in free time, seemed quite surprising at first. The moments when a person is in a high-challenge, high-skill situation, accompanied by feelings of concentration, creativity, and satisfaction, were reported more often at work than at home. After further thought, however, this finding is not that surprising. What often passes unnoticed is that work is much more like a game than most other things we do during the day. It usually has clear goals and rules of performance. It provides feedback either in the form of knowing that one has finished a job well done, in terms of measurable sales, or through an evaluation by one's supervisor. A job usually encourages concentration and prevents distractions; it also allows a variable amount of control, and—at least ideally—its difficulties match the worker's skills. Thus work tends to have the structure of other intrinsically rewarding activities that provide flow, such as games, sports, music, and art. In comparison, much of the rest of life lacks these elements. When spending time at home with the family or alone, people often lack a clear purpose, do not know how well they are doing, are distracted, feel that their skills are underutilized, and as a result feel bored or—more rarely—anxious.

So it is no wonder that the quality of experience at work is generally more positive than one would expect. Nevertheless, if we had the chance we would like to work less. Why is this so? Two major reasons seem to be involved. The first is based on the objective conditions of work. It is true that since time immemorial those who paid another person's wages were not particularly concerned with the well-being of their employees. It takes extraordinary inner resources to achieve flow while digging a mile below ground in a South African mine, or cutting sugarcane on a sweltering plantation. Even in our enlightened days, with all the emphasis on "human resources," management is all too often disinterested in how employees experience work. Therefore it is not surprising that many workers assume that they cannot count on work to provide the intrinsic rewards in their lives, and that they have to wait until they are out of the factory or office before they can begin to have a good time—even though this turns out not to be true.

The second reason is complementary to the first one, but is based less on contemporary reality, and more on the historical disrepute of work, which is still transmitted by the culture and learned by each of us as we grow up. There is no question that during the Industrial Revolution of two and a half centuries ago factory workers had to labor under inhuman conditions. Free time was so rare that it became one of the most precious of commodities. Workers assumed that if only they had more of it, they would automatically be happier. The trade unions fought heroically to shorten the work week, and their success is one of the bright accomplishments in the history of humankind. Unfortunately, while free time might be a necessary condition for happiness, by itself it is not sufficient to guarantee it. Learning how to use it beneficially turns out to be more difficult than expected. Nor does it seem that more of a good thing is necessarily better; as is true of so many other things, what enriches life in small quantities might impoverish it in larger doses. This is why by mid-century psychiatrists and sociologists were putting up warning signals to the effect that too much free time was threatening to become a social disaster.

Both of these reasons—the objective work environments and the subjective attitudes we learn toward them—conspire to make it difficult for many persons to admit, even to themselves, that work can be enjoyable. Yet when approached without too many cultural prejudices and with a determination to shape it so as to make it personally meaningful, even the most mundane job can enhance the quality of life, rather than detract from it.

But of course the intrinsic rewards of work are easiest to see in the highly individualized professions, where a person is free to choose his or her goals and set the difficulty of the task. Highly productive and creative artists, entrepreneurs, statesmen, and scientists tend to experience their jobs like our hunting ancestors did theirs—as completely integrated with the rest of their lives. One of the most common tropes in the nearly hundred interviews I conducted with such persons as Nobel Prize–winners and other creative leaders in different fields was: "You could say that I worked every minute of my life, or you could say with equal justice that I never worked a day." The historian John Hope Franklin expressed this blending of work and leisure most concisely when he said: "I have always subscribed to the expression: 'Thank God it's Friday' because to me Friday means I can work for the next two days without interruptions."

For such individuals, flow is a constant part of their professional activity. Even though operating at the edges of knowledge must necessarily include much hardship and inner turmoil, the joy of extending the mind's reach into new territories is the most obvious feature of their lives, even past the age when most people are usually content to retire. The inventor Jacob Rabinow, with over two hundred patents to his name, describes his work at age eighty-three: "You have to be willing to pull the ideas, because you're interested. . . . [P]eople like myself like to do it. It's fun to come up with an idea, and if nobody wants it, I don't give a damn. It's just fun to come up with something strange and different."

Ed Asner of "Lou Grant" fame was still looking for new challenges to his acting skills at age sixty-three: "I thirst to

. . . burst at the seams, eager for the chase." The double Nobel laureate Linus Pauling, interviewed when he was eighty-nine, said: "I don't think I ever sat down and asked myself, now what am I going to do in life? I just went ahead doing what I liked to do." The eminent psychologist Donald Campbell advised young scholars: "Don't go into science if you are interested in money. Don't go into science if you will not enjoy it even if you do not become famous. Let fame be something that you accept graciously if you get it, but make sure that it is a career that you can enjoy." And Mark Strand, former poet laureate of the United States, describes flow well in the pursuit of his vocation: "you're right in the work, you lose your sense of time, you're completely enraptured, you're completely caught up in what you are doing . . . when you are working on something and you are working well, you have the feeling that there's no other way of saying what you're saying."

Of course, people like these are very fortunate in having attained the pinnacle of glamorous professions. But it would also be easy to find a great number of famous and successful people who hate their jobs, whereas one can find businessmen, plumbers, ranchers, and even assembly-line workers who love their work and describe it in lyrical terms. It is not the external conditions that determine how much work will contribute to the excellence of one's life. It is how one works, and what experiences one is able to derive from confronting its challenges.

No matter how satisfying, work alone cannot make a life complete. Most creative individuals we interviewed said that their families were more important to them than their careers—even though their actual habits often belied these sentiments. Stable, emotionally rewarding marriages were the norm among them. When asked what accomplishments in life they were most proud of, one of the most typical responses echoed that of the physicist Freeman Dyson: "I suppose it is just to have raised six kids, and brought them up, as far as one can see, all to be interesting people. I think that's what I am most proud of, really." John Reed, CEO of Citicorp, claimed that the best investment he ever made was the year he took off from his successful career to spend with his children as they were growing up: "Raising kids is far more rewarding than earning money for a company, in terms of a sense of satisfaction." And most such individuals fill whatever free time they have with interesting leisure activities, from playing public concerti to collecting rare nautical maps, from taking up cooking and cookbook writing to volunteering to teach in underdeveloped countries.

Thus love and dedication to one's calling does not have to have the negative connotations of "workaholism." That term could legitimately be applied to a person who is so immersed in work as to give up other goals and responsibilities. A workaholic runs the risk of seeing only the challenges related to his job, and learning only the skills appropriate to it; he is unable to experience flow in any other activity. Such a person misses a great deal of the opportunities that contribute to the excellence of life, and often ends life miserably, when after an all-consuming addiction to work, he is left with nothing he can do. Fortunately there are many examples of persons who, although dedicated to their work, have more multifaceted lives.

FIVE

The Risks and Opportunities of Leisure

It sounds somewhat ridiculous to say that one of the problems we face at this point in history is that we haven't learned how to spend free time in a sensible way. Yet this is a concern that many have expressed ever since the mid-century. In 1958, the Group for the Advancement of Psychiatry ended its annual report with the conclusion: "For many Americans, leisure is dangerous." Others have claimed that whether America succeeds as a civilization will depend on the way we use free time. What could justify such grave warnings? But before answering this question about the effects of leisure on society, it makes sense to reflect on how a typical person is affected by leisure. The historical effects in this case are the sum of individual experiences, so in order to understand the former it helps to understand the latter.

For a variety of reasons discussed earlier, we have come to assume that free time is one of the most desirable goals we can aspire to. While work is seen as a necessary evil, being able to relax, to have nothing to do, seems to most people the royal road to happiness. The popular assumption is that no skills are involved in enjoying free time, and that anybody can do it. Yet the evidence suggests the opposite: free time is more difficult to enjoy than work. Having leisure at one's disposal does not improve the quality of life unless one knows how to use it effectively, and it is by no means something one learns automatically.

The psychoanalyst Sandor Ferenczi at the turn of the century already noticed that on Sundays his patients came down with bouts of hysteria and depression more often than during the rest of the week; he called the syndrome "Sunday neurosis." Ever since, it has been reported that holidays and vacations are periods of increased mental disturbance. For workers who have identified with their jobs all their lives, retirement is often a transition to chronic depression. In our ESM studies we find that even physical health is better when a person focuses on a goal. On weekends, when alone, and with nothing to do, people report more symptoms of illness.

All of this evidence points to the fact that the average person is ill equipped to be idle. Without goals and without others to interact with, most people begin to lose motivation and concentration. The mind begins to wander, and more often than not it will focus on unresolvable problems that cause anxiety. In order to avoid this undesirable condition, the person resorts to strategies that will ward off the worst of psychic entropy. Without necessarily being aware of it, one will seek out stimulation that will screen out the sources of anxiety from consciousness. This might be watching TV, or reading redundant narratives such as romances or mysteries, or engaging in obsessive gambling or promiscuous sexuality, or getting drunk or taking drugs. These are quick ways to reduce chaos in consciousness in the short run, but usually the only residue they leave behind is a feeling of listless dissatisfaction.

Apparently, our nervous system has evolved to attend to external signals, but has not had time to adapt to long periods without obstacles and dangers. Few people have learned to structure their psychic energy autonomously, from the inside. In those successful societies where adults had time on their hands, elaborate cultural practices evolved to keep the mind busy. These included complex cycles of ceremonial rituals, dancing, and competitive tournaments that occasionally lasted for days and weeks on end—such as the Olympic games that started toward the dawn of European history. Even if lacking religious or aesthetic activities, at least each village provided endless opportunities for gossip and discussion; under the largest tree of the square, men not otherwise occupied sat smoking their pipes or chewing mildly hallucinogenic leaves and nuts, and kept their minds ordered through redundant conversation. This is still the pattern followed by men at leisure in the coffee shops of the Mediterranean, or the beer halls of northern Europe.

Such methods of avoiding chaos in consciousness work to a certain extent, but they rarely contribute to a positive quality of experience. As we have seen earlier, human beings feel best in flow, when they are fully involved in meeting a challenge, solving a problem, discovering something new. Most activities that produce flow also have clear goals, clear rules, immediate feedback—a set of external demands that focuses our attention and makes demands on our skills. Now these are exactly the conditions that are most often lacking in free time. Of course, if one uses leisure to engage in a sport, an art form, or a hobby, then the requirements for flow will be present. But just free time with nothing specific to engage one's attention provides the opposite of flow: psychic entropy, where one feels listless and apathetic.

Not all free-time activities are the same. One major distinction is between active and passive leisure, which have quite different psychological effects. For example, U.S. teenagers experience flow (defined as high-challenge, high-skill moments) about 13 percent of the time that they spend watching television, 34 percent of the time they do hobbies, and 44 percent of the time they are involved in sports and games (see table 4). This suggests that hobbies are about two and a half times more likely to produce a state of heightened enjoyment than TV does, and active games and sports about three times more. Yet these same teenagers spend at least four times more of their free hours watching TV than doing hobbies or sports. Similar ratios are also true for adults. Why would we spend four times more time doing something that has less than half the chance of making us feel good?

When we ask the participants of our studies this question, a consistent explanation begins to appear. The typical teenager admits that biking, or playing basketball, or playing the piano are more enjoyable than roaming through the mall or watching TV. But, they say, to get organized for a basketball game takes time—one has to change clothes, make

Table 4
How Much Flow Is There in Leisure?

Percentage of time each leisure activity provides flow, relaxation, apathy, and anxiety. Results are from a study of 824 U.S. teenagers yielding about 27,000 responses. Terms are defined as follows: Flow: high challenges, high skills; Relaxation: low challenges, high skills; Apathy: low challenges, low skills; and Anxiety: high challenges, low skills.

	Flow	Relaxation	Apathy	Anxiety
Games and sports	44	16	16	24
Hobbies	34	30	18	19
Socializing	20	39	30	12
Thinking	19	31	35	15
Listening to music	15	43	35	7
Television watching	13	43	38	6

Source: Bidwell, Csikszentmihalyi, Hedges, and Schneider 1997, in press.

arrangements. It takes at least half an hour of often dull practice each time one sits down at the piano before it begins to be fun. In other words, each of the flow-producing activities requires an initial investment of attention before it begins to be enjoyable. One needs such disposable "activation energy" to enjoy complex activities. If a person is too tired, anxious, or lacks the discipline to overcome that initial obstacle, he or she will have to settle for something that, although less enjoyable, is more accessible.

This is where "passive leisure" activities come in. To just hang out with friends, read an unchallenging book, or turn on the TV set does not require much in the way of an upfront energy outlay. It does not demand skills or concentration. Thus the consumption of passive leisure becomes all too often the option of choice, not only for adolescents, but for adults as well.

In table 4, we can see a comparison of the major types of leisure activities in terms of how frequently they provide flow to a cross section of American teenagers. We see that games and sports, hobbies, and socializing—the three active and/or social activities—provide more flow experiences than the three more solitary and less structured activities, listening to music, thinking, and watching TV. At the same time, the activities that produce flow, being more demanding and difficult, also occasionally produce conditions of anxiety. The three passive leisure activities, on the other hand, seldom cause anxiety: their contribution is to provide mainly relaxation and apathy. If you fill your leisure time with passive leisure you won't find much enjoyment, but you will also avoid getting in over your head. Apparently this is a bargain that many find worth making.

It is not that relaxing is bad. Everyone needs time to unwind, to read trashy novels, to sit on the couch staring in space or watching a TV program. As with the other ingredients of life, what matters is the dosage. Passive leisure becomes a problem when a person uses it as the principal—or the only—strategy to fill up free time. As these patterns turn into habits, they begin to have definite effects on the quality of life as a whole. Those who learn to rely on gambling to pass the time, for instance, may find themselves caught in a habit that interferes with their job, their family, and eventually with their own well-being. People who view television more often than the average tend also to have worse jobs and worse relationships. In a large-scale study in Germany, it was found that the more often people report reading books, the more flow experiences they claim to have, while the opposite trend was found for watching television. The most flow was reported by individuals who read a lot and watched little TV, the least by those who read seldom and watched often.

Of course, such correlations do not necessarily mean that habits of passive leisure cause bad jobs, bad relationships, and so on. It is likely that the causal links start from the other end: lonely people with dissatisfying jobs will fill their free time with passive leisure. Or those who cannot find flow otherwise in their lives turn to undemanding leisure activities. But in human development causation is usually circular: what was an effect in the beginning eventually turns into a cause. An abusive parent may force his child to adopt a defense based on repressed aggression; as the child grows up, it is this style of defense rather than the initial trauma that might make it easy for him in turn to become an abusive parent. So adopting habits of passive leisure is not just an effect of previous problems, but becomes a cause in its own right, which cuts off further options for improving the quality of life.

The phrase "bread and circuses" has become a commonplace to describe how the Roman Empire managed to keep the populace contented during the long centuries of its decline. By providing enough food to keep the bodies satisfied, and enough spectacles to keep the minds entertained, the ruling classes were able to avoid social unrest. It is unlikely that this policy was consciously adopted, but its widespread application seems to have worked. It would not have been either the first or the last time that providing leisure opportunities kept a community from unraveling. In the *Persian Wars*, the first historian of the West, the Greek Herodotus, describes how Atys, king of Lydia in Asia Minor, introduced ball games some three thousand years ago as a way to distract his subjects when a series of bad crops caused unrest in the hungry population. "The plan adopted against the famine was to engage in games one day so entirely as not to feel any craving for food" he wrote, "and the next day to eat and abstain from games. In this way they passed eighteen years."

A similar pattern developed in Constantinople during the waning of the Byzantine Empire. To keep the citizens happy, great chariot races were held in the city. The best drivers became rich and famous, and they were automatically elected to the Senate. In Central America before the Spanish conquest, the Maya developed elaborate games similar to basketball, which kept spectators busy for weeks on end. In our times, disenfranchised minorities depend on sports and entertainment as avenues to social mobility—basketball, baseball, boxing, and popular music absorb surplus psychic energy while promising wealth and fame. Depending on one's perspective, one can interpret this in two quite opposite ways. One can see in these instances leisure being used as an "opiate of the masses," to paraphrase what Marx said about religion. Or one can see them as creative responses to dangerous situations impervious to more effective solutions.

The record seems to suggest that a society begins to rely heavily on leisure—and especially on passive leisure—only when it has become incapable of offering meaningful productive occupation to its members. Thus "bread and circuses" is a ploy of last resort that postpones the dissolution of society only temporarily. Contemporary examples provide some insight into what happens in such instances. For example, many indigenous people in North America have lost the opportunity to experience flow in work and communal life, and seek to recapture it in leisure activities that mimic the earlier enjoyable lifestyle. Young Navajo men used to feel at their best when riding after their sheep over the mesas of the Southwest, or when participating in week-long ceremonial singing and dancing. Now that such experiences are less relevant, they attempt to recapture flow by drinking alcohol and then racing down the desert highways in souped-up cars. The number of traffic fatalities may not be higher than those sustained earlier in tribal warfare or while shepherding, but they seem more pointless.

The Inuit are going through a similar dangerous transition. Young people who can no longer experience the excitement of hunting seal and trapping bear turn to the automobile as a tool for escaping boredom and focusing on a purposeful goal. Apparently there are communities in the Arctic that have no roads connecting them to any other place, but have built miles of roads for the exclusive purpose of drag racing. In Saudi Arabia the spoiled young scions of oil barons find riding camels passé, and try to revive their interest by racing brand-new Cadillacs in the trackless desert, or on the sidewalks of Riyadh. When productive activities become too routine and meaningless, leisure will pick up the slack. It will take up progressively more time, and rely on increasingly more elaborate artificial stimulation.

There are individuals who, confronted with the sterility of their jobs, escape productive responsibilities altogether to pursue a life of flow in leisure. This does not necessarily require a great deal of money. There are well-trained engineers who leave their jobs and wash dishes in restaurants during the winter so they can afford to do rock climbing all summer. There are colonies of surfers on all the beaches with good waves who live hand-to-mouth so they can cram in as much flow as possible on their boards.

An Australian social scientist, Jim Macbeth, interviewed dozens of ocean sailors who spend year after year navigating among the islands of the South Pacific, many of them owning nothing except the boat into which they've invested all their savings. When they run out of money for food or repairs, they stop in a port to do odd jobs until they can replenish their supplies, then they cast off on the next journey. "I was able to throw off responsibility, cast off a humdrum life, be a bit adventurous. I had to do something with life besides vegetate," says one of these modern argonauts. "It was a chance to do one really big thing in my life; big and memorable," says another. Or, in the words of another sailor:

> Modern civilization has found radio, TV, nightclubs and a huge variety of mechanized entertainment to titillate our senses and help us escape from the apparent boredom of the earth and the sun and wind and stars. Sailing returns to these ancient realities.

Some individuals do not abandon jobs altogether, but shift the emphasis from work to leisure as the center of their lives. One serious rock climber describes the exhilarating self-discipline of his sport as training for the rest of life: "If you win these battles enough, that battle against yourself . . . it becomes easier to win the battles in the world." And another former businessman who moved to the mountains to be a carpenter:

> I would have made a great deal of money in corporate life, but I realized one day that I wasn't enjoying it. I wasn't having the kind of experiences that make life rewarding. I saw that my priorities were mixed up, spending most of my hours in the office. . . . The years were slipping by. I enjoy being a carpenter. I live where it's quiet and beautiful, and I climb most every night. I figure that my own relaxation and availability will mean more to my family than the material things I can no longer give them.

The career move from businessman to carpenter is an example of the kind of creative readjustment that some people are able to bring to their lives. They search until they find a productive endeavor that also allows them to build as much flow as possible into their lives. The other options seem less satisfying; there is just too much one misses by becoming a workaholic, or by escaping into leisure full time. Most of us, however, are content to compartmentalize our lives into boring jobs and routine entertainment. An interesting example of how flow seeps out of work and into leisure is provided in the study of an Alpine community by Antonella Delle Fave and Fausto Massimini of the University of Milan. They interviewed forty-six members of an extended family in Pont Trentaz, a remote mountain village where people have cars and television sets, but still work at traditional tasks such as herding cattle, growing orchards, and woodworking. The psychologists asked the three generations of villagers to describe when and how they experienced flow in their lives (see figure 2).

Figure 2
Distribution of Flow Activities in a Three-Generational Family (N=46) from Pont Trentaz, Gressoney Valley, Italy

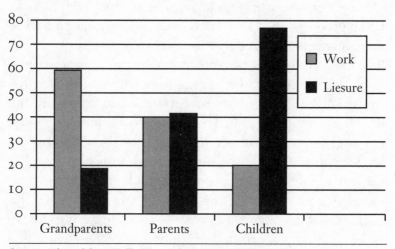

Source: Adapted from Delle Fave and Massimini 1988.

The oldest generation reported the most frequent flow experiences, and the majority of them involved work: cutting hay in the meadows, fixing the barn, baking bread, milking cows, working in the garden. The middle generation—which included those between forty and sixty years old—reported equal amounts of flow from work and from leisure activities, such as watching movies, going on vacations, reading books, or skiing. The grandchildren in the youngest generation showed a pattern opposite to that of their grandparents: they reported the fewest occurrences of flow, and most of it came from leisure. Dancing, motorcycle racing, and watching TV were some of the most frequent avenues of enjoyment. (Figure 2 does not show how much flow each group reported; it only shows the percentage of flow that was reported in either work or leisure.)

Not all of the generational differences in Pont Trentaz are due to social change. Some of it is a feature of normal developmental patterns that every generation passes through: young people are always more dependent for enjoyment on artificial risk and stimulation. But it is almost certain that these normal differences are magnified in communities undergoing social and economic transition. In such cases the older generations still find a meaningful challenge in traditional productive tasks, whereas their children and grandchildren, increasingly bored by what they see as irrelevant chores, turn to entertainment as a way of avoiding psychic entropy.

In the United States, traditional communities like the Amish and the Mennonites have been able to keep work and flow from getting separated. In the everyday routines of their farming life, it is difficult to know when work stops and leisure begins. Most "free time" activities, such as weaving, carpentry, singing, or reading are useful and productive either in a material, social, or spiritual sense. Of course this achievement has been at the price of remaining embalmed in amber, as it were, arrested at a point of technological and spiritual development that now seems quaint. Is this the only way to preserve the integrity of a joyful and productive existence? Or is it possible to reinvent a lifestyle that combines these traits within continuing evolutionary change?

To make the best use of free time, one needs to devote as much ingenuity and attention to it as one would to one's job. Active leisure that helps a person grow does not come easy. In the past leisure was justified because it gave people an opportunity to experiment and to develop skills. In fact, before science and the arts became professionalized, a great deal of scientific research, poetry, painting, and musical composition was carried out in a person's free time. Gregory Mendel did his famous genetic experiments as a hobby; Benjamin Franklin was led by interest, not a job description, to grind lenses and experiment with lightning rods; Emily Dickinson wrote her superb poetry to create order in her own life. Nowadays only experts are supposed to be interested in such issues; amateurs are derided for venturing into fields reserved for the specialist. But amateurs—those who do something because they love to do it—add enjoyment and interest to their own life, and to everybody else's.

It is not just extraordinary individuals who are able to make creative use of leisure. All folk art—the songs, the fabrics, the pottery and carvings that give each culture its particular identity and renown—is the result of common people striving to express their best skill in the time left free from work and maintenance chores. It is difficult to imagine how dull the world would be if our ancestors had used free time simply for passive entertainment, instead of finding in it an opportunity to explore beauty and knowledge.

Currently about 7 percent of all the nonrenewable energy we use—electricity, gasoline, paper, and metal products—is being used primarily for leisure. Constructing and watering golf courses, printing magazines, flying jets to vacation resorts, producing and distributing TV shows, building and fueling powerboats and skidoos takes up a good deal of planetary resources. Ironically, it seems that how much happiness and enjoyment we get from leisure has no relation at all—if anything, a *negative* relation—to the amount of material energy consumed while doing it. Low-key activities that require investments of skill, knowledge, and emotions on our part are just as rewarding as those that use up a lot of equipment and external energy, instead of our own psychic energy. Having a good conversation, gardening, reading poetry, volunteering in a hospital, or learning something new exhaust few resources and are at least as enjoyable as things that consume ten times as many resources.

Just as the excellence of an individual life depends to a large extent on how free time is used, so the quality of a society hinges on what its members do in their leisure time. Suburban communities can be so depressingly bland because one has reason to believe that behind the impressive facades rising from the emerald lawns nobody is doing anything interesting. There are entire countries where one gets the impression from talking even with members of the societal elite that besides money, family, fashion, vacations, and gossip there is not that much else that engages their attention. Whereas there are still some areas in the world where one finds retired professionals enchanted with classical poetry who collect ancient volumes in their library, or farmers who play musical instruments or write down the stories of their village, preserving the best creations of their ancestors while adding to them.

In any case, we have seen that at the social as well as the individual level habits of leisure act as both effects and as causes. When the lifestyle of a social group becomes obsolete, when work turns into a boring routine and community responsibilities lose their meaning, it is likely that leisure will become increasingly more important. And if a society becomes too dependent on entertainment, it is likely that there will be less psychic energy left to cope creatively with the technological and economic challenges that will inevitably arise.

It may seem contrarian to raise alarms about the entertainment industry at a time when it is so successful in the U.S.

Music, movies, fashion, and television bring in hard currency from all over the world. Video stores mushroom on practically every block, reducing the ranks of the unemployed. Our children look to media celebrities as models to steer their lives by, and our consciousness is filled with information about the doings of athletes and movie stars. How can all this success be harmful? If we assess trends only from the point of view of a financial bottom line, then there is nothing wrong. But if one counts also the long-term effects of generations addicted to passive entertainment, the rosy picture will look grim indeed.

How to avoid the danger of polarizing life into work that is meaningless because it is unfree, and leisure that is meaningless because it has no purpose? One possible way out is suggested by the example of the creative individuals discussed in the previous chapter. In their lives, work and play are indivisible, as they are for people living in traditional societies. But unlike the latter, creative persons have not retrenched into a frozen moment in time. They use the best knowledge from the past and the present to discover a better way of being in the future. To the extent that we can learn from them, there is no longer any reason to dread free time. Work itself becomes as enjoyable as leisure, and when one needs a break from it, leisure is likely to be true recreation instead of a scheme for dulling the mind.

If one's job is beyond redemption, the other solution is to make sure that free time at least will be a real opportunity for flow—for exploring the potential of the self and the environment. Luckily, the world is absolutely full of interesting things to do. Only lack of imagination, or lack of energy, stand in the way. Otherwise each of us could be a poet or musician, an inventor or explorer, an amateur scholar, scientist, artist, or collector.

SIX

Relationships and the Quality of Life

When thinking about what causes the best and the worst moods in life, chances are you would think of other people. A lover or spouse can make you feel wonderfully elated but also irritated and depressed; children can be a blessing or a pain; a word from the boss can make or break a day. Of all the things we normally do, interaction with others is the least predictable. At one moment it is flow, the next apathy, anxiety, relaxation, or boredom. Because of the power that interactions have on our mind, clinicians have developed forms of psychotherapy that depend on maximizing pleasant encounters with others. There is no doubt that well-being is deeply attuned to relationships, and that consciousness resonates to the feedback we receive from other people.

For example, Sarah, one of the people we studied with the Experience Sampling Method, at 9:10 on a Saturday morning was sitting alone in her kitchen, having breakfast and reading the paper. When the pager signaled, she rated her happiness 5 on a scale where 1 is sad and 7 very happy. When the next signal arrived at 11:30, she was still alone, smoking a cigarette, saddened by the thought that her son was about to move away to a different city. Now her happiness had fallen to a 3. At 1:00 in the afternoon, Sarah was alone, vacuuming the living room, happiness down to 1. By 2:30 P.M. she is in the backyard, swimming with the grandchildren; happiness is a perfect 7. But less than an hour later, as she is taking the sun and trying to read a book while her grandchildren splash her with water, the happiness rating is down to 2 again: "My daughter-in-law should take those brats in hand more," she writes on the ESM response sheet. As we move through the day, thinking about people and interacting with them play constant riffs on our moods.

In most societies, people depend on the social context to an even greater extent than in the technological West. We believe that the individual should be left free to develop his or her potential, and at least since Rousseau we have come to think of society as a perverse obstacle to personal fulfillment. In contrast, the traditional view, especially in Asia, has been that the individual is nothing until shaped and refined through interaction with others. India provides one of the clearest examples of how this works. The classical Hindu culture has taken great pains to ensure that from infancy to old age its members conform to appropriate ideals of behavior. "The Hindu person is produced consciously and deliberately during a series of collective events. These events are *samskaras*, life cycle rituals that are fundamental and compulsory in the life of a Hindu," writes Lynn Hart. *Samskaras* help to shape children and adults by giving them new rules of conduct for each successive step in life.

As the Indian psychoanalyst Sadhir Kakar wrote half facetiously, *samskaras* are the right rite at the right time:

The conceptualization of the human life cycle unfolding in a series of stages, with each stage having its unique "tasks" and the need for an orderly progression through the stages, is an established part of traditional Indian thought . . . one of the major thrusts of these rituals is the gradual integration of the child into society, with the *samskaras*, as it were, beating time to a measured movement that takes the child away from the original mother-infant symbiosis into the full-fledged membership of his community.

But socialization not only shapes behavior, it also molds consciousness to the expectations and aspirations of the culture, so that we feel shame when others observe our failings, and guilt when we feel that we have let others down. Here too cultures differ enormously in terms of how deeply the self depends on internalized community expectations; for instance, the Japanese have several words to describe fine shadings of dependence, obligations, and responsibility that are difficult to translate into English because in our social environment we have not learned to experience such feelings to the same extent. In Japan, according to Shintaro Ryu, a perceptive Japanese journalist, the typical individual "wants to go wherever others go; even when he goes to the beach to swim, he avoids the uncrowded place but chooses a spot where people are practically on top of one another."

It is not difficult to see why we are so enmeshed in our social milieu, both mentally and physically. Even our primate relations, the apes that live in the African jungles and savannas, have learned that unless they are accepted by the group they won't live long; a solitary baboon will soon fall prey to leopards or hyenas. Our ancestors realized a long time ago that they were social animals, that they depended on the group not only for protection but also for learning the amenities of life. The Greek word "idiot" originally meant someone who lived by himself; it was assumed that cut off from community interaction such a person would be mentally incompetent. In contemporary preliterate societies this knowledge is so deeply ingrained that a person who likes to be alone is assumed to be a witch, for a normal person would not choose to leave the company of others unless forced to do so.

Because interactions are so important for keeping consciousness in balance, it is important to understand how they affect us, and to learn how to turn them into positive rather than negative experiences. As with everything else, one cannot enjoy relationships for free. We must expend a certain amount of psychic energy to reap their benefits. If we do not, we risk finding ourselves in the shoes of Sartre's character in *No Exit* who concluded that hell was other people.

A relationship that leads to order in consciousness instead of psychic entropy has to meet at least two conditions. The first is to find some compatibility between our goals and that of the other person or persons. This is always difficult in principle, given that each participant in the interaction is bound to pursue his or her self-interest. Nevertheless, in most situations, if one looks for it, one can discover at least a shred of shared goals. The second condition for a successful interaction is that one be willing to invest attention in the other person's goals—not an easy task either, considering that psychic energy is the most essential and scarce resource we own. When these conditions are met, it is possible to get the most valuable result from being with other people—to experience the flow that comes from optimal interaction.

The most positive experiences people report are usually those with friends. This is especially true for adolescents (see figure 3), but it remains true also in the later years of life. People are generally much happier and more motivated when with friends, regardless of what they are doing. Even studying and household chores, which depress moods when done alone or with the family, become positive experiences when done with friends. It is not difficult to see why this should be the case. With friends the conditions for an optimal interaction are usually maximized. We choose them because we see their goals as compatible with ours, and the relationship is one of equality. Friendships are expected to provide mutual benefits, with no external constraints that might lead to exploitation. Ideally, friendships are never static: they provide ever new emotional and intellectual stimulation, so that the relationship does not fade into boredom or apathy. We try new things, activities, and adventures; we develop new attitudes, ideas, and values; we get to know friends more deeply and intimately. While many flow activities are enjoyable only in the short run, because their challenges are soon exhausted, friends offer potentially infinite stimulation throughout life, honing our emotional and intellectual skills.

Of course, this ideal is not achieved very often. Instead of promoting growth, friendships often provide a safe cocoon where our self-image can be preserved without ever having to change. The superficial sociability of teenage peer groups, suburban clubs and coffee klatches, professional associations, drinking buddies, gives a soothing sense of being part of a like-minded set of people without demanding effort or growth. One indication of this trend is shown in figure 3, where we see that concentration is usually significantly lower with friends than in solitude. Apparently mental effort is rarely involved in typical friendly interactions.

In the worst cases, when a person without other close ties comes to depend exclusively on other rootless individuals for emotional support, friendship can be destructive. Urban gangs, delinquent groups, and terrorist cells are usually made up of individuals who—either because of their own fault or because of circumstances—have not found a niche in any community and have only each other to confirm their identities. In such cases growth also happens as a result of the relationship, but from the point of view of the majority it is a malignant growth.

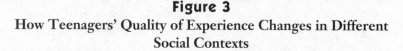

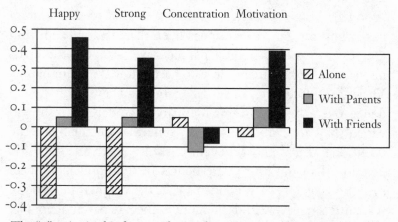

The "o" point in this figure refers to the average quality of experience reported throughout the week. The feelings of happiness and strength are very significantly worse alone, and better with friends; motivation is very significantly better with friends. Similar trends are obtained from all ESM studies, whether with adults or teenagers, in this country or abroad.

Source: Csikszentmihalyi and Larson 1984.

Compared to the other main features of the social environment, however, friendships offer both the most emotionally rewarding contexts in the immediate present, and the greatest opportunities for developing one's potential in the long run. Contemporary life, however, is not very suitable for sustaining friendships. In more traditional societies a person remains in contact throughout all of his or her life with the friends made in childhood. The geographical and social mobility in the United States makes this almost impossible. Our high school friends are not the same as those we made in grade school, and in college friendships are reshuffled once more. Then one moves from one job to another, from one city to the next, and with age, transient friendships become ever more superficial. Lack of true friends is often the main complaint of people confronting an emotional crisis in the second half of life.

Another frequent cause of complaint is the lack of rewarding sexual relationships. One of the cultural achievements of
this century has been the rediscovery of the importance of
"good sex" for a good life. However, as usual, the pendulum
has swung too far: sexuality has been decontextualized from
the rest of experience, and people have accepted the erroneous notion that liberal doses of sex will make them happy.
Variety and frequency of sexual encounters have taken precedence over the depth and intensity of the relationship in
which they are embedded. It is ironic that on this issue the
traditional teachings of the churches are closer to a scientific
position than the up-to-date beliefs of the populace, for an
evolutionary approach confirms that the original purpose of
sexuality is making children and binding the parental couple.
Of course this does not mean that these functions need to be
the only purpose of sex. For example, the adaptive function
of taste buds was to distinguish between wholesome and
spoiled food, but with time we developed complex culinary
arts based on subtle nuances of taste. So also whatever were
the original reasons for sexual pleasure, it can always be used
to yield new possibilities for enriching life. But just as glut-
tony that has no relationship to hunger seems unnatural, an
obsession with sex that is divorced from other human needs
such as intimacy, caring, and commitment becomes equally
aberrant.

When the daring pioneers of instinctual liberation hailed
free sex as the solution to the repression of society, they did
not dwell on the possibility that half a century later sex would
be used to sell deodorants and soft drinks. As Herbert Marcuse and others ruefully noted, Eros was bound to be exploited one way or another; its energy was too strong for it
not to be co-opted by the powers of church, state, or if neither of these, then the advertising industry. In the past, sexuality was repressed so that the psychic energy attracted to it
could be channeled into productive goals. Now sexuality is
encouraged so that people will channel their psychic energy

into consumption that gives them the illusion of sexual fulfillment. In either case, a force that could result in some of
the deepest and most intimate joys of life is taken over and
manipulated by outside interests.

What can one do? As with other aspects of life, the important thing is to decide for oneself, to realize what is at stake,
and what are the interests that try to control our sexuality for
their own ends. It helps to realize how vulnerable we are in
this respect. It is a very universal condition: we were told in
our part of the Rockies that coyotes sometimes send a female
in heat to lure unsuspecting male farm dogs into the ambush
of the pack. When realizing our vulnerability, the danger is
falling into the opposite extreme and becoming paranoid
about sex. Neither celibacy nor promiscuity are necessarily
to our advantage; what counts is how we wish to order our
lives, and what part we wish sexuality to play in it.

In partial compensation for the difficulty of having friends,
we have discovered in the United States a new possibility: to
be friends with parents, spouses, and children. In the European tradition of courtly love, friendship with one's husband
or wife was considered an oxymoron. When marriages were
largely at the service of economic or political alliances, and
children depended on their parents for inheritance and sta-
tus, the conditions of equality and reciprocity that make
friendships possible were lacking. In the last few generations,
however, the family has lost most of its role as an economic
necessity. And the less we depend on it for material benefits,
the more we can enjoy its potential for emotional rewards.
Thus the modern family, with all its problems, opens up new
possibilities for optimal experiences that were much more
difficult to come by in previous times.

In the last few decades, we have come to realize that the
image of the family we have been cherishing since at least
Victorian times is only one of many possible alternatives. According to the historian Le Roy Ladurie, a rural French fam-

ily in the late Middle Ages was made up by whoever lived under the same roof and shared the same meals. This might have included people actually related by blood, but also farmhands and other persons who strayed in to help with the farm work and were given shelter. Apparently no further distinction was made among these individuals; whether related or not they were seen to belong to the same *domus*, or house made of stone and mortar, which was the unit that really mattered, rather than the biological family. A thousand years earlier, the Roman family was a very different social arrangement. Here the patriarch had the legal right to kill his children if they displeased him, and biological descent mattered almost as much as it did later for the aristocratic families of the nineteenth century.

And these variations were still within the same cultural tradition. In addition, anthropologists have made us familiar with a huge variety of other family forms, from the enormously extended Hawaiian family where every woman of the older generation is considered to be one's "mother," to various forms of polygamous and polyandrous arrangements. All of which has prepared us to see the dissolution of the nuclear family, with 50 percent divorce rates and the majority of children growing up in father-absent or reconstituted families, as not so much a tragedy as a normal transition to new forms adapted to changing social and economic conditions. At the extremes, we hear claims that the family is an obsolete, reactionary institution destined to disappear.

An opposite view is proposed by conservatives who aim to uphold "family values," meaning a return to the conventional patterns enshrined in mid-century television sitcoms. Who is right in this controversy? Clearly both sides are right to some extent, and both are wrong in taking a rigid view of an evolving pattern. On the one hand, it is disingenuous to argue that an ideal family pattern ever existed, and that we can hold on to this chimera while the rest of social conditions are changing. On the other hand it is equally mistaken to argue that a healthy social system can exist without the emotional support and nurturance that parents alone seem able to give growing children. For no matter how much variety there is in the form families have taken, one constant has been that they included adults of the opposite sex who took on responsibilities for each others' welfare, and for that of their offspring.

It is for this reason that marriage is such a complex institution in all societies. The negotiations involved in it, which have included fine calculations of dowries and bride-price, were intended to guarantee that children born of the union would not become a public burden. In all societies, the parents and relatives of the bride and groom took on the responsibility of supporting and training the offspring of the union, both in terms of material needs and of socialization into community values and rules. So far no society—not the Soviet Union, not Israel, not Communist China—has been able to finesse the family and substitute other social institutions in its stead. It is one of the great ironies of our times that with all good intentions liberal capitalism has succeeded in weakening families more than they ever had been before—without being able to invent a substitute for them.

The effects of family relationships on the quality of life are so extensive that volumes could be written about it. In fact many great works of literature, from *Oedipus Rex* to *Hamlet*, *Madame Bovary* to *Desire Under the Elms* have it as their theme. Family interactions affect the quality of experience in different ways for each member. Fathers, mothers, and children will respond to the same event according to their perception of the situation, and the history of past vicissitudes in their relationship. But to make a very broad generalization, the family acts as a flywheel for the emotional ups and downs of the day. Moods at home are rarely as elated as with friends, and rarely as low as when one is alone. At the same time, it is at home that one can release pent-up emotions with relative safety, as shown by the unfortunate abuse and violence that are a feature of dysfunctional families.

In an extensive study of family dynamics with the Experience Sampling Method, Reed Larson and Maryse Richards found several interesting patterns. For instance, when both parents are employed, husbands' moods are low at work, but improve when they get home, while the opposite is true for wives who have to face household chores when they return from the outside job, thus creating opposite cycles of emotional well-being. Contrary to what one would expect, there are more arguments in families that are emotionally close; when the family is in real trouble, parents and children avoid each other instead of arguing. Even in contemporary families gender differences among the spouses are still strong: the moods of the father affect the moods of the rest of the family, and the children's moods affect the mother, but the mothers' moods have little discernible effect on the rest of the family. Also, about 40 percent of the fathers and less than 10 percent of the mothers say that their teenagers' achievement puts them in a good mood; whereas 45 percent of the mothers and only 20 percent of the fathers say that the teenagers' being in a good mood improves their own. Clearly men are still more concerned about what their children do, and women about how their children feel, as gender roles require.

Much has been written about what makes families work. The consensus is that families that support the emotional well-being and growth of their members combine two almost opposite traits. They combine discipline with spontaneity, rules with freedom, high expectations with unstinting love. An optimal family system is complex in that it encourages the unique individual development of its members while uniting them in a web of affective ties. Rules and discipline are needed to avoid excessive waste of psychic energy in the negotiation of what can or cannot be done—when the children should come home, when to do homework, who is to wash the dishes. Then the psychic energy released from bickering and arguing can be invested in the pursuit of each member's goals. At the same time, each person knows that he or she can draw on the collective psychic energy of the family if needed. Growing up in a complex family, children have a chance to develop skills and recognize challenges, and thus are more prepared to experience life as flow.

In our society, the average person spends about one-third of his or her waking time alone. Persons who spend much more or much less time by themselves often have problems. Teenagers who always hang out with peers have trouble in school and are unlikely to learn to think for themselves, while those who are always alone are easy prey to depression and alienation. Suicide is more frequent among people whose work isolates them physically, such as lumbermen in the North, or emotionally, like psychiatrists. The exceptions involve situations where the days are so strictly programmed that psychic entropy has no chance to take hold of consciousness. Chartousian monks may spend most of their lives in their secluded cells without ill effects, or, at the other extreme of sociability, the same is true of submarine crews, where the sailors might never have any privacy for months on end.

In many preliterate societies, the optimal amount of solitude was zero. The Dobuans of Melanesia described by the anthropologist Reo Fortune are typical in that they tried to avoid being alone like the plague. In Dobu, when people had to go into the bush to relieve themselves, they always went with a friend or relative, for fear of being harmed by witchcraft if they went alone. That sorcery is most effective against a lonely person is not an entirely fanciful idea. What it describes is a real fact, although its explanation is allegorical. It describes what many social scientists have noted, namely that the mind of a solitary individual is vulnerable to delusions and irrational fears. When we talk to another person, even about the most trivial subjects such as the weather or last night's ball game, the conversation introduces a shared reality into our consciousness. Even a greeting such as "Have a nice day" reassures us that we exist because other people notice us, and are concerned about our welfare. Thus the fundamental function of even the most routine encounters is *reality maintenance*, which is indispensable, lest consciousness disintegrate into chaos.

In line with such reasons, people in general report much lower moods when alone than when they are with others. They feel less happy, less cheerful, less strong, and more bored, more passive, more lonely. The only dimension of experience that tends to be higher alone is concentration. When first hearing about these patterns, many thoughtful persons are incredulous: "This cannot be true," they say, "*I* love to be alone and seek out solitude when I can." In fact it is possible to learn to like solitude, but it does not come easily. If one is an artist, scientist, or writer; or if one has a hobby, or a rich inner life, then being alone is not only enjoyable but necessary. Relatively few individuals, however, master the mental tools that will make this possible.

Most people also overestimate their ability to tolerate solitude. A survey conducted in Germany by Elizabeth Noelle-Neumann shows the amusing lengths to which we go to delude ourselves in this respect. She showed thousands of respondents two pictures of a mountain landscape. One picture featured a meadow crowded with hikers, the other the same scene but with only a few people. Then she asked two questions. The first was: "In which of these two places would you prefer to spend your holidays?" About 60 percent chose the deserted meadow and only 34 percent the crowded one. The second question was: "In which of these two places do you think most Germans would prefer to spend their holidays?" To this, 61 percent answered that the crowded scene would be their compatriots' first choice, and 23 percent the lonely one. Here as in many similar situations, one can learn more about true preferences by listening to what people say others want, rather than to what they claim they want themselves.

Whether we like solitude or not, however, in our times we must be able to put up with some of it. It is difficult to learn math, or practice the piano, or program a computer, or figure out the purpose of one's life when other people are around. The concentration required to order thoughts in consciousness is easily interrupted by an extraneous word, by the necessity to pay attention to another person. Thus we find that adolescents who feel that they must always be with friends—and these are usually youngsters whose families provide little emotional support—tend not to have the psychic energy necessary for complex learning. Even with superior mental aptitude, the dread of solitude prevents them from developing their talents.

If it is true that loneliness has been a constant threat to humankind, strangers have been no less of a problem. Generally we assume that people who differ from us—by kinship, language, race, religion, education, social class—will have goals at cross-purposes from ours, and therefore must be watched with suspicion. Early human groups usually assumed that they were the only true humans, and those who did not share their culture were not. Even though genetically we are all related, cultural differences have served to reinforce our isolation from each other.

Because of this, whenever different groups have come into contact, they have been all too often able to ignore each other's humanity and treat the "Other" as an enemy that in case of need could be destroyed without too much compunction. This is true not only of headhunters in New Guinea, but of Bosnian Serbs and Muslims, Irish Catholics and Protestants, and an infinity of other conflicts between races and creeds barely simmering under the surface of civilization.

The first real melting pots of diverse tribal identities were the great cities that arose about eight thousand years ago in many different parts of the world, from China to India to

Egypt. Here for the first time people from different backgrounds learned to cooperate and to tolerate foreign ways. But even the cosmopolitan metropolis has been unable to eliminate the fear of strangers. In medieval Paris, students as young as seven years old had to wear daggers when they walked to and from the cathedral schools, to defend themselves against kidnappers and thieves; now students in the inner city wear guns. In the seventeenth century, it was extremely common for women walking the city streets to be raped by gangs of roaming youth. In the urban jungle, a man with a different skin color, different clothes and demeanor is still a potential predator.

In this case too, however, there is another side to the coin. For while we are repelled by differences, we are also fascinated by the strange and the exotic. The metropolis is so attractive in part because the clash of cultures sets up an atmosphere of excitement, freedom, and creativity that is difficult to find in an isolated, homogeneous culture. As a result, people report some of their most positive experiences in public spaces where they are surrounded by strangers—parks, streets, restaurants, theaters, clubs, and beaches. As long as we can presume that the "Others" will share our basic goals, and will behave predictably within certain limits, their presence adds a great deal of spice to the quality of life.

The current push toward pluralism and a global culture (admittedly not the same thing, but both tending toward integration rather than differentiation) is one way to reduce the strangeness of strangers. Another is the "restoration" of communities. The quotation marks in the previous sentence are there to indicate that ideal communities, like ideal families, may never have really existed. When reading histories of private lives, one is hard put to find any place, at any time, where people went about their business in serene cooperation, without fear of enemies from inside or outside the community. There might have been no racial minorities or organized crime in small Chinese, Indian, or European towns, but one found misfits, deviants, heretics, inferior castes, political or religious animosities that exploded in civil war, and so on. In the United States the earliest communities must have had a great deal of cohesion—provided they were not split by witch hunts, Indian wars, conflicts between those for and against the British Crown, or for and against slavery.

In other words, the ideal community that inspired Norman Rockwell's brushes was no more typical than his pink, well-fed families sitting with bowed heads and complacent smiles around the Thanksgiving dinner table. Nevertheless, this does not mean that trying to create wholesome communities is a bad idea. Rather, it suggests that instead of looking for models in the past, we should figure out what a safe yet stimulating social environment could be like in the future.

From the beginnings of Western philosophy, thinkers have conceived of two main ways of fulfilling human potentials. The first involved the *vita activa*, or the expression of one's being through action in the public arena—paying attention to what goes on in the social environment, making decisions, engaging in politics, arguing for one's convictions, taking a stand even at the cost of one's comfort and reputation. This is what some of the most influential Greek philosophers saw as the ultimate fulfillment of one's essence. Later, under the influence of Christian philosophy, the *vita contemplativa* gained ascendancy as the best way to spend one's life. It was through solitary reflection, prayer, communion with the supreme being, that one was thought to achieve the most complete fulfillment. And these two strategies were usually seen as mutually exclusive—one could not be a doer and a thinker at the same time.

This dichotomy still pervades our understanding of human behavior. Carl Jung introduced the concepts of extroversion versus introversion as fundamental and opposite traits of the psyche. The sociologist David Riesman described a historical change from inner-directed to outer-

directed personalities. In current psychological research, extroversion and introversion are considered the most stable
personality traits that differentiate people from each other
and that can be reliably measured. Usually each of us tends
to be one or the other, either loving to interact with people
but feeling lost when alone, or finding delight in solitude but
unable to relate to people. Which one of these types is the
most likely to get the best out of life?

Current studies provide consistent evidence that outgoing,
extroverted people are happier, more cheerful, less stressed,
more serene, more at peace with themselves than introverts.
The conclusion seems to be that extroverts—who are
thought to be born, not made—get a better deal in life all-
around. In this case, however, I have some reservations about
how the data have been interpreted. One of the manifestations of extroversion is to put a positive spin on things, while
introverts are more prone to be reserved in describing their
inner states. So the quality of experience might be similar in
both groups, and only the reporting differs.

A better solution is suggested by the study of creative individuals. Instead of being either extroverts or introverts, such
people seem to express both traits in the process of going
about their lives. True, the stereotype of the "solitary genius" is strong and does have a basis in fact. After all, one
must generally be alone in order to write, paint, or do experiments in a laboratory. Yet over and over again creative individuals stress the importance of seeing people, hearing
people, exchanging ideas, and getting to know another person's work. The physicist John Archibald Wheeler expresses
this point with great directness: "If you don't kick things
around with people, you are out of it. Nobody, I always say,
can be anybody without somebody being around."

Another outstanding scientist, Freeman Dyson, expresses
with a fine nuance the opposite phases of this dichotomy in
his work. He points to the door of his office and says:

Science is a very gregarious business. It is essentially the difference between having this door open and having it shut. When I am doing science I have the door open. . . . You want to be, all the time, talking with people . . . because it is only by interacting with other people that you get anything interesting done. It is essentially a communal enterprise. There are new things happening all the time, and you should keep abreast and keep yourself aware of what is going on. You must be constantly talking. But, of course, writing is different. When I am writing I have the door shut, and even then too much sound comes through, so very often when I am writing I go and hide in the library. It is a solitary game.

John Reed, the CEO of Citicorp who has led his company successfully through some turbulent times, has built the alternation between inner-directed reflection and intense social interaction into his daily routine:

I'm an early morning guy. I get up at 5 always, get out of the shower about 5:30, and I typically try to work either at home or at the office, and that's when I do a good bit of my thinking and priority setting. . . . I try to keep a reasonably quiet time until 9:30 or 10:00. Then you get involved in lots of transactions. If you are chairman of the company it's like being a tribal chieftain. People come into your office and talk to you.

Even in the very private realm of the arts the ability to interact is essential. The sculptor Nina Holton describes well the role of sociability in her work:

You really can't work entirely alone in your place. You want to have a fellow artist come and talk things over with you: "How does that strike you?" You have to have some sort of feedback. You can't be sitting there entirely by yourself. . . . And then eventually, you know, when you begin to show, you have to have a whole network. You have to get to know gallery people, you have to get to know people who work in your field who are involved. And you may want to find out whether you wish to be part of it or not be part of it, but you cannot help being part of a fellowship, you know?

The way these creative individuals confront life suggests that it is possible to be both extroverted and introverted at the same time. In fact, expressing the full range from inner- to outer-directedness might be the normal way of being human. What is abnormal is to get boxed in at one of the ends of this continuum, and experience life only as a gregarious, or only as a solitary being. Certainly temperament and socialization will push us in one or the other direction, and after a while it becomes easy to fall in with these conditioning forces and learn to relish either social interaction or solitude, but not both. To do so, however, curtails the full range of what humans can experience, and diminishes the possibilities of enjoyment in life.

SEVEN

Changing the Patterns of Life

A few years ago, an eighty-three-year-old man wrote one of the most touching letters I have ever received from a reader. After World War I, he wrote, he had been a soldier in the field artillery, stationed in the South. They used horses to pull the gun carriages, and after maneuvers they often unhitched them and played games of polo. During those games he felt an exhilaration that he had never felt before or after; he assumed that only playing polo could make him feel so good. The next sixty years were routine and uneventful. Then he read *Flow*, and realized that the thrill he had experienced as a young man on horseback was not necessarily limited to the game of polo, and began to do some things he had thought might be fun to do, but never tried. He took up gardening, listening to music, and other activities that, lo and behold, revived the excitement of his youth.

It is good that in his eighties this man had discovered that

97

he need not accept passively a boring life. Still, the intervening sixty years seem to have been unnecessarily barren. And how many people never realize that they can shape their psychic energy so as to get the most out of experience? If the finding that about 15 percent of the population are never in flow is accurate, that means that just in this country tens of millions of people are depriving themselves of what makes life worth living.

Of course, in many cases one can well understand why a person may experience flow rarely, or not at all. A deprived childhood, abusive parents, poverty, and a host of other external reasons may make it difficult for a person to find joy in everyday life. On the other hand, there are so many examples of individuals who overcame such obstacles that the belief that the quality of life is determined from the outside is hardly tenable. Some of the most vocal disagreements to what I have written about flow came from readers who claimed to have been abused, and who wanted me to know that contrary to what I had said, it was perfectly possible for abused children to enjoy their adult lives.

Examples are too many to mention. One of my favorites involves Antonio Gramsci, the philosopher of humanistic socialism that had such a strong influence on the development of European thought in this century, and on the eventual demise of Leninism-Stalinism. Born in 1891 to a destitute family on the poor island of Sardinia, Antonio had a deformed spine and was sickly all through childhood. Their poverty became almost intolerable when his father, arrested on false charges, was imprisoned and could no longer support his large family. In an unsuccessful attempt to cure his hunchback, Antonio's uncle would hang the child by his ankles from the rafters of the hovel in which they lived. Antonio's mother was so sure that the child was eventually going to pass away in his sleep that every night she set out his one good suit and a pair of candles on the dresser so that the funeral preparations would take less time. Given these facts, it would have come as no surprise that Gramsci grew up full of hatred and spite. Instead he dedicated his life to helping the oppressed, by becoming a subtle writer and brilliant theoretician. Although one of the founders of the Italian Communist Party, he never compromised his humanitarian values for the sake of expediency or party dogma. Even after Mussolini had him imprisoned in a medieval jail so that he would die in solitary confinement, he kept writing letters and essays full of light, hope, and compassion. All of the external factors conspired to twist Gramsci's life; he must take all the credit for achieving the intellectual and emotional harmony that he left as his heritage.

Another example, from my own researches this time, concerns the life of Linus Pauling. He was born in Portland, Oregon, at the turn of the century; his father died when Linus was nine years old, leaving the family impoverished. Although he was an omnivorous reader and collected minerals, plants, and insects, Linus did not think he would go past high school. Fortunately, the parents of one of his friends almost forced him to enroll in college. Then he received a scholarship to get into Cal Tech, became involved in research, was awarded the Nobel prize in chemistry in 1954, and the Nobel peace prize in 1962. He describes his college years as follows:

> I made a little money by odd jobs, working for the college, killing dandelions on the lawn by dipping a stick in a bucket containing sodium arsenate solution and then stabbing the stick into the dandelion plant. Every day I chopped wood, a quarter of a cord perhaps, into lengths— they were already sawed—into a size that would go into the wood-burning stoves in the girls' dormitory. Twice a week I cut up a quarter of a beef into steaks or roasts, and every day I mopped the big kitchen, the very large kitchen area. Then at the end of my sophomore year, I got a job as a paving engineer, laying blacktop pavement in the mountains of Southern Oregon.

What was so amazing about Linus Pauling is that even at ninety years of age he kept the enthusiasm and curiosity of a young child. Everything he did or said was bubbling with energy. Despite the early adversity and the later hardships, he exuded an obvious joie de vivre. And there was no secret about how he did it; in his own words: "I just went ahead doing what I liked to do."

Some will find such an attitude irresponsible: how can someone afford the self-indulgence of doing only what he likes to do? But the point is that Pauling—and the many others who share his attitude—like to do almost everything, no matter how difficult or trivial, including the things they are forced to do. The only thing they definitely don't like is wasting time. So it is not that their life is objectively better than yours or mine, but that their enthusiasm for it is such that most of what they do ends up providing them with flow experiences.

Recently there has been a lot written about how people are born either with a happy or a sad temperament, and there is not that much one can do to change it. If you happen to be a happy person, you will stay that way no matter how much bad luck you encounter. If you are not, a strike of good luck may lift your mood for a short while, but you will soon return to the lukewarm, average moroseness doomed by the genes. If this were true, then it would be hopeless to try changing the quality of one's life. But this deterministic scenario is correct only insofar as the extroverted exuberance that is often mistaken for happiness is concerned. That seems indeed to be a fairly stable trait of a person's character. It is a different story, however, if by happiness we mean the less obvious enjoyment of life that flow provides.

In a rare ESM longitudinal study of teenagers, for instance, Joel Hektner found that about 60 percent of the adolescents reported the same frequency of flow over a one-week period measured two years apart; those who had much of it earlier still had it later, and those who had little early had little two years later. But the remaining 40 percent changed over the same period, half reporting significantly more flow (measured as high-challenge, high-skill experiences), half less. Those whose frequency of flow increased two years later spent more time studying and less in passive leisure, and their levels of concentration, self-esteem, enjoyment, and interest was significantly higher than that of the teenagers whose frequency of flow decreased—although two years earlier the two groups had reported the same quality of experience. It is important to note that the teens whose flow increased did not report being "happier" than the ones who decreased. But because of the great differences in the other dimensions of experience, it is safe to conclude that the happiness reported by the low flow group was more shallow and less authentic. This suggests that it is indeed possible to improve the quality of one's life by investing psychic energy in activities that are more likely to produce flow.

Because for most of us a job is such a central part of life, it is essential that this activity be as enjoyable and rewarding as possible. Yet many people feel that as long as they get decent pay and some security, it does not matter how boring or alienating their job is. Such an attitude, however, amounts to throwing away almost 40 percent of one's waking life. And since no one else is going to take the trouble of making sure that we enjoy our work, it makes sense for each of us to take on this responsibility.

Generally there are three main reasons that jobs are resented. The first is that the job is pointless—it does no good to anyone, and in fact it may be harmful. Some government employees, high-pressure salesmen, and even scientists working in fields like armaments or the tobacco industry have to engage in some heavy denial to tolerate what they do for a living. The second reason is that the work is boring and routine; it provides no variety or challenge. After a few years, one can do it in one's sleep, and all it provides is a feeling of stagnation rather than growth. The third problem with jobs is that they are often stressful; especially when one can't get along with one's supervisor or colleagues who expect too much or do not recognize one's contributions. Contrary to popular opinion, concerns for more money and security are usually not as important as these three in determining whether one will be satisfied with one's job or not.

Even if we don't want to admit it, the ability to overcome most obstacles is within our hands. We can't blame family, society, or history if our work is meaningless, dull, or stressful. Admittedly, there are not too many options when we realize that our job is useless, or actually harmful. Perhaps the only choice is to quit as quickly as possible, even at the cost of severe financial hardship. In terms of the bottom line of one's life, it is always a better deal to do something one feels good about than something that may make us materially comfortable but emotionally miserable. Such decisions are notoriously difficult, and require great honesty with oneself. As Hannah Arendt has shown with regard to Adolf Eichmann and the other employees of the Nazi extermination camps, it is easy to disguise the responsibility for even the cold-blooded murder of thousands with the excuse: "I only work here."

The psychologists Ann Colby and William Damon have described many individuals who have gone to extreme lengths to make their work meaningful, people who have left a "normal" existence in order to dedicate themselves to making a difference in the lives of others. One such person is Susie Valdez, who was drifting from one low-paying and boring service job to another on the West Coast, with no prospects for anything better. Then during a visit to Mexico she saw the garbage hills at the outskirts of Ciudad Juarez, where hundreds of homeless urchins survived by scavenging. Susie found here people who were even more desperate than she was, and discovered she had the power to show the children a better way to live; she built a mission house among the refuse, started a school and a clinic, and became known as the "Queen of the Dumps."

Short of making such a dramatic switch, there are a great many ways to make one's job more meaningful by adding value to it. A supermarket clerk who pays genuine attention to customers, a physician concerned about the total well-being of patients rather than specific symptoms only, a news reporter who considers truth at least as important as the sensational interest when writing a story, can transform a routine job with ephemeral consequences into one that makes a difference. With increasing specialization, most occupational activities have become repetitive and one-dimensional. It is difficult to build a positive self-concept if all one does is stock supermarket aisles or fill out forms from morning to night. By taking the whole context of the activity into account, and understanding the impact of one's actions on the whole, a trivial job can turn into a memorable performance that leaves the world in a better shape than it was before.

Like everyone else, I could make a long list of encounters with workers who, in addition to doing their job, helped reduce entropy around them. A service station attendant who fixed a windshield wiper with a smile and refused to be paid for such a minor effort; a real-estate salesman who kept helping years after he sold the house; a flight attendant who was willing to stay after the rest of the crew left the airport to locate a missing wallet . . . In all such cases, the value of the job performance was increased because the worker was willing to invest extra psychic energy into it, and thus was able to withdraw from it additional meaning. But the meaning we derive from a job does not come free. As these examples show, one must do some thinking and caring beyond what the job description calls for. And this in turn requires additional attention, which, as has been said again and again, is the most precious resource we have.

A similar argument holds for turning a job that lacks challenge and variety into one that satisfies our need for novelty and achievement. Here too one needs to expend additional psychic energy to reap the desired benefits. Without some effort a dull job will just stay dull. The basic solution is quite simple. It involves paying close attention to each step involved in the job, and then asking: Is this step necessary? Who needs it? If it is really necessary, can it be done better, faster, more efficiently? What additional steps could make my contribution more valuable? Our attitude to work usually involves spending a lot of effort trying to cut corners and do as little as possible. But that is a short-sighted strategy. If one spent the same amount of attention trying to find ways to accomplish more on the job, one would enjoy working more—and probably be more successful at it, too.

Even some of the most important discoveries come about when the scientist, paying attention to a routine process, notices something new and unusual that needs to be explained. Wilhelm C. Roentgen discovered radiation when he noticed that some photographic negatives showed signs of being exposed even in the absence of light; Alexander Fleming discovered penicillin when he noticed that bacterial cultures were less dense on dishes that had not been cleaned and were moldy; Rosalyn Yalow discovered the radioimmunoassay technique after she noticed that diabetics absorbed insulin slower than normal patients, instead of faster, as it had been assumed. In all these cases—and the records of science are full of similar ones—a humdrum event is transformed into a major discovery that changes the way we live because someone paid more attention to it than the situation seemed to warrant. If Archimedes, lowering himself into the bath, had only thought, "Darn, I got the floor wet again, what will the missus say?" humankind might have had to wait another few hundred years to understand the principle of fluid displacement. As Yalow describes her own experience: "Something comes up, and you recognize that it has happened." Sounds simple, but most of us are usually too distracted to recognize when something happens.

As minute changes can result in great discoveries, so small adjustments can turn a routine job one dreads into a professional performance one can look forward to with anticipation each morning. First, one must pay attention so as to understand thoroughly what is happening and why; second, it is essential not to accept passively that what is happening is the only way to do the job; then one needs to entertain alternatives and to experiment with them until a better way is found. When employees are promoted to more challenging positions, it is usually because they followed these steps in their previous jobs. But even if no one else notices, the worker who uses psychic energy this way will have a more satisfying job.

One of the clearest examples I have ever seen was when I did research in a factory where audiovisual equipment was being assembled on a production line. Most of the workers on the line were bored and looked down on their job as something beneath them. Then I met Rico, who had a completely different take on what he was doing. He actually thought his job was difficult, and that it took great skill to do it. It turned out he was right. Although he had to do the same sort of boring task as everyone else, he had trained himself to do it with the economy and the elegance of a virtuoso. About four hundred times each day a movie camera would stop at his station, and Rico had forty-three seconds to check out whether the sound system met specifications. Over a period of years, experimenting with tools and patterns of motion, he had been able to reduce the average time it took him to check each camera to twenty-eight seconds. He was as proud of this accomplishment as an Olympic athlete would be if, after the same number of years spent preparing, he could break the forty-four second mark in the 400 meter sprint. Rico did not get a medal for his record, and reducing the time to do his job did not improve production, because the line still kept moving at the old speed. But he loved the exhilaration of using his skills fully: "It's better than anything else—a whole lot better than watching TV." And because he sensed that he was getting close to his limit in the present job, he was taking evening courses for a diploma that would open up new options for him in electronic engineering.

It will come as no surprise that the same type of approach is needed for solving the problem of stress at work, since stress is detrimental to achieving flow. In common usage, the word "stress" applies both to the tension we feel, and to its external causes. This ambiguity leads to the erroneous assumption that external stress must inevitably result in psychic discomfort. But here again, there is no one-to-one relation between the objective and the subjective; external stress (which to avoid confusion we might call "strain") need not lead to negative experiences. It is true that people feel anxious when they perceive the challenges in a situation as far exceeding their skills, and that they want to avoid anxiety at all cost. But the perception of challenges and skills rests on a subjective evaluation that is amenable to change.

At work, there are as many sources of strain as there are in life itself: unexpected crises, high expectations, insoluble problems of all sorts. How does one keep them from becoming stressful? A first step consists in establishing priorities among the demands that crowd into consciousness. The more responsibilities one has, the more essential it becomes to know what is truly important and what is not. Successful people often make lists, or flowcharts of all the things they have to do, and quickly decide which tasks they can delegate, or forget about, and which ones they have to tackle personally, and in what order. Sometimes this activity takes the form of a ritual, which like all rituals serves in part as a reassurance that things are under control. John Reed, CEO of Citicorp, spends time each morning setting his priorities. "I am a great lister," he says, "I have twenty lists of things to do all the time. If I ever have five free minutes I sit and make lists of things that I should be worrying about. . . ." But it is not necessary to be so systematic; some people trust their memory and experience, and make their choices more intuitively. The important thing is to develop a personal strategy to produce some kind of order. After priorities are set, some people will confront first the easiest tasks on the list and clear the desk for the more difficult ones; others proceed in reverse order because they feel that after dealing with the tough items the easier ones will take care of themselves. Both strategies work, but for different people; what's important is for each person to find out which one fits best.

Being able to create order among the various demands that crowd upon consciousness will go a long way toward preventing stress. The next step is to match one's skills with whatever challenges have been identified. There will be tasks we feel incompetent to deal with—can they be delegated to someone else? Can you learn the skills required in time? Can you get help? Can the task be transformed, or broken up into simpler parts? Usually the answer to one of these questions will provide a solution that transforms a potentially stressful situation into a flow experience. None of this will happen, however, if one responds to the strain passively, like a rabbit frozen by the headlights of an oncoming car. One must invest attention into the ordering of tasks, into the analysis of what is required to complete them, into the strategies of solution. Only by exercising control can stress be avoided. And while everyone has the psychic energy needed to cope with strain, few learn to use it effectively.

The careers of creative individuals give some of the best examples of how one can shape work to one's own requirements. Most creative persons don't follow a career laid out for them, but invent their job as they go along. Artists invent their own style of painting, composers their own musical styles. Creative scientists develop new fields of science, and make it possible for their successors to have careers in them. There were no radiologists before Roentgen, and there was no nuclear medicine before Yalow and her colleagues pioneered that field. There were no auto workers before entrepreneurs like Henry Ford built up the first production lines.

Obviously very few people can start entirely new lines of work; most of us will follow the job description of conventional careers. But even the most routine job can benefit from the kind of transforming energy that creative individuals bring to what they do.

George Klein, a tumor biologist who heads a renowned research department at the Karolinska Institute in Stockholm, illustrates well how such people approach their work. Klein likes what he does enormously, yet there are two aspects of his job that he hates. One is waiting at airport terminals, which he has to do often because of his very busy schedule of international meetings. The other aspect he detests is writing the inevitable grant proposals to government agencies that provide the funding for his research team. These two boring tasks were depleting his psychic energy, and building up dissatisfaction with his work. Yet they could not be avoided. Then Klein had a flash of inspiration: What if he combined these two tasks? If he could write his grant applications while waiting for planes, he would save half the time previously devoted to boring tasks. To implement this strategy he bought the best pocket tape recorder he could find, and started to dictate grant proposals while waiting or inching forward at airport customs lines. These aspects of his job are still objectively what they were before, but because he took control Klein transformed them almost into a game. It is now a challenge to dictate as much as possible while waiting, and instead of feeling that he is wasting time at a boring task, he feels energized.

On every airline flight one sees dozens of men and women working on their laptop computers, or adding columns of figures, or highlighting technical articles they are reading. Does it mean that like George Klein they feel energized by having combined travel with work? It depends on whether they feel obliged to do so, or whether they have adopted this strategy to save time or gain efficiency. In the first case, working on the plane is likely to be stressful rather than flow-producing. If it is something one feels one has to do, it would perhaps be better to look at the clouds below, read a magazine, or chat with a fellow passenger instead.

Besides work, the other major area that impacts on the quality of life is the kind of relationships we have. And there is often a conflict between these two, so that a person who loves work may neglect family and friends, and vice versa. The inventor Jacob Rabinow, in describing how his wife feels often ignored, echoes what all people devoted to their work would say:

> I'm so involved in an idea I'm working on, I get so carried away, that I'm all by myself. I'm not listening to what anybody says. . . . [Y]ou're not paying attention to anybody. And you tend to drift away from people. . . . [I]t could be that if I were not an inventor but had a routine job, I'd spend more time at home and I'd pay more attention to them. . . . So maybe people who don't like their jobs love their home more.

There is quite a bit of truth to this remark, and the reason is simple. Given that attention is a limited resource, when one goal takes up all our psychic energy, there is none left over.

Nevertheless, it is difficult to be happy if one neglects either one of these two dimensions. Many people married to their jobs are aware of it, and find ways of compensating either by choosing an understanding spouse, or by being very careful in rationing their attention. Linus Pauling was very open about this issue: "I was fortunate, I believe, that my wife felt her duty in life and her pleasure in life would come from her family—her husband and children. And that the way she could best contribute would be to see to it that I would not be bothered by the problems involved in the household; that she would settle all of these problems in such a way that I could devote all of my time to my work." But few people—and especially few women—could call themselves as fortunate as Pauling in this respect.

A more realistic venue is to find ways to balance the meaningfulness of the rewards we get from work and from relationships. For despite the fact that almost everyone claims the family is the most important concern in their lives, very few—especially few men—behave as if this were the case. True, most married men are convinced that their lives are dedicated to the family, and from a material standpoint this might be true. But it takes more than food in the fridge and two cars in the garage to keep a family going. A group of people is kept together by two kinds of energy: material energy provided by food, warmth, physical care, and money; and the psychic energy of people investing attention in each other's goals. Unless parents and children share ideas, emotions, activities, memories, and dreams, their relationship will survive only because it satisfies material needs. As a psychic entity, it will exist only at the most primitive level.

Amazingly enough, many people refuse to see this point. The most widespread attitude seems to be that as long as material needs are provided for, a family will take care of itself; it will be a warm, harmonious, permanent refuge in a cold and dangerous world. It is very common to meet successful men in their late forties and fifties who are stunned when their wives suddenly leave or their children get into serious trouble. Didn't they always love their family? Didn't they invest all their energy to make them happy? True, they never had more than a few minutes each day to talk, but how could they have done otherwise, with all the demands from the job . . .

The usual assumption we make is that to achieve career success requires a great deal of continuous investment of thought and energy. Family relationships, by contrast, are "natural," so they demand little mental effort. A spouse will continue to be supportive, children will keep minding their parents—more or less—because that is how families are supposed to be. Businessmen know that even the most successful company needs constant attention, because external and internal conditions are always changing, and need to be adjusted to. Entropy is a constant factor, and if it is not attended to, the company will dissolve. Yet many of them assume that families are somehow different—entropy cannot touch them and so they are immune to change.

There were some grounds for such a belief when families were kept together by external bonds of social control, and by internal bonds of religious or ethical commitment. Contractual obligations have the advantage of making relationships predictable and saving energy by excluding options and the need for constant negotiation. When marriage was supposed to be forever, it did not need constant effort to maintain. Now that the integrity of the family has become a matter of personal choice, it cannot survive except through the regular infusion of psychic energy.

The new kind of family is very vulnerable unless it can provide intrinsic rewards to its members. When family interaction provides flow, it is in the self-interest of everyone to continue the relationship. Yet because families are taken so much for granted, few people have learned to transform the old ties that bound because of external obligations into new ones that hold because of the enjoyment they provide. When parents come home exhausted from their jobs they hope that being with the family will be an effortless, relaxing, invigorating experience. But to find flow in family relations requires as much skill as in any other complex activity.

The Canadian author Robertson Davies describes one of the reasons his marriage of fifty-four years has been so rewarding:

Shakespeare has played an extraordinary role in our marriage as a source of quotations and jokes and references, which are fathomless. I feel that I am uncommonly lucky because we've had such a terribly good time together. It's always been an adventure and we haven't come to the end yet. We haven't finished talking, and I swear that conversation is more important to marriage than sex.

For Davies and his wife, the skill that made joint flow possible was a common love and knowledge of literature. But one could substitute almost anything for Shakespeare. A couple in their sixties revived their relationship by starting to run marathons together; others have done it through travel, gardening, or breeding dogs. When people pay attention to each other, or to the same activity together, the chances of flow binding the family increases.

Parenting is supposed to be one of the most rewarding experiences in life; but it isn't, unless one approaches it with the same attention as one would a sport or an artistic performance. In a study of flow in motherhood, Maria Allison and Margaret Carlisle Duncan described several examples of how the psychic energy invested in a child's growth can produce enjoyment in parenting. Here a mother describes the times she achieves flow:

> . . . when I'm working with my daughter; when she's discovering something new. A new cookie recipe that she has accomplished, that she has made herself, and artistic work that she has done that she's proud of. Her reading is one thing that she's really into, and we read together. She reads to me, and I read to her, and that's a time when I sort of lose touch with the rest of the world, I'm totally absorbed in what I'm doing. . . .

To experience such simple pleasures of parenting, one has to pay attention, to know what the child is "proud of," what she is "into"; then one has to devote more attention to share those activities with her. Only when there is harmony between the goals of the participants, when everyone is investing psychic energy into a joint goal, does being together become enjoyable.

The same holds true for any other type of interaction. For instance, when there is reason to think that we are appreciated, job satisfaction is usually high; whereas the greatest source of stress in the workplace is the feeling that no one is interested in supporting our goals. Infighting among coworkers, inability to communicate with superiors and subordinates are the bane of most jobs. The roots of interpersonal conflict are often an excessive concern for oneself, and an inability to pay attention to the needs of others. It is sad to see how often people ruin a relationship because they refuse to recognize that they could serve their own interests best by helping others achieve theirs.

In American corporate culture, the hero is a ruthless, competitive person with a huge ego. Unfortunately some top entrepreneurs and CEOs do conform to that image. Yet it is also reassuring that aggressive selfishness is not the only path to success. In fact in most stable and well-run companies, leaders try to promote subordinates who don't invest all their psychic energy in self-advancement, but use some of it to advance corporate goals. They know that if top management is filled with greedy egotists the company will eventually suffer for it.

Keith is one example of many managers I have met who have spent a decade or more desperately trying to impress their superiors in order to get promoted. He worked seventy hours and more a week even when he knew it was not necessary, neglecting his family and his own personal growth in the process. To increase his competitive advantage Keith hoarded all the credit he could for his accomplishments, even if it meant making colleagues and subordinates look bad. But despite all his efforts, he kept being passed over for important promotions. Finally Keith resigned himself to having reached the ceiling of his career, and decided to find his rewards elsewhere. He spent more time with the family, took up a hobby, became involved in community activities. Because he was no longer struggling so hard, his behavior on the job became more relaxed, less selfish, more objective. In fact, he began to act more like a leader whose personal agenda takes second place to the well-being of the company. Now the general manager was finally impressed. This is the kind of person we need at the helm. Keith was promoted soon after he had let go of his ambition. His case is by no means rare: To be trusted in a position of leadership, it helps to advance other people's goals as well as one's own.

Congenial relations on the job are important, but the quality of life depends also on innumerable encounters with other people outside of work. This is not as simple as it sounds: each time we stop to speak to another person it takes up some psychic energy, and we become vulnerable to being ignored, ridiculed, or exploited. Most cultures develop their own peculiar patterns for facilitating social interaction. In groups where kinship is the main principle of organization, you may be expected to joke with your sisters-in-law but never talk to your mother-in-law. In traditional hierarchical societies like that of ancient China, complex forms of greetings and conventional conversational formulae insured that people could communicate without having to waste time figuring out what to say and how to say it. Americans have perfected a form of easy conversation that fits the mobile and democratic nature of our society; its superficial heartiness, however, is just as formulaic as those of an African tribe. To gain something from talking to a person, one has to learn something new, either in knowledge or emotions. That requires both participants to concentrate on the interaction, which in turn demands psychic energy that generally we are unwilling to invest. Yet a genuine flow of conversation is one of the highlights of existence.

The secret of starting a good conversation is really quite simple. The first step is to find out what the other person's goals are: What is he interested in at the moment? What is she involved in? What has he or she accomplished, or is trying to accomplish? If any of this sounds worth pursuing, the next step is to utilize one's own experience or expertise on the topics raised by the other person—without trying to take over the conversation, but developing it jointly. A good conversation is like a jam session in jazz, where one starts with conventional elements and then introduces spontaneous variations that create an exciting new composition.

If work and relationships are able to provide flow, the quality of everyday life is bound to improve. But there are no gimmicks, no easy shortcuts. It takes a total commitment to a fully experienced life, one in which no opportunities are left unexplored and no potential undeveloped, to achieve excellence. The organization of the self that makes this possible is the topic of the next chapter.

EIGHT

The Autotelic
Personality

Other things being equal, a life filled with complex flow activities is more worth living than one spent consuming passive entertainment. In the words of a woman describing what her career means to her: "To be totally absorbed in what you are doing and to enjoy it so much that you don't want to be doing anything else. I don't see how people survive if they don't experience something like that. . . ." Or as the historian C. Vann Woodward says of his work, which involves trying to understand the dynamics of the American South:

It interests me. It is a source of satisfaction. Achieving something that one thinks is important. Without such a consciousness or motivation it seems to me that life could be rather dull and purposeless, and I wouldn't want to attempt that kind of life. Of complete leisure, say, of having

116

absolutely nothing to do that one felt was worth doing—that strikes me as a rather desperate situation to be in.

When we are able to confront life with such involvement and enthusiasm, we can be said to have achieved an autotelic personality.

"Autotelic" is a word composed of two Greek roots: *auto* (self), and *telos* (goal). An autotelic activity is one we do for its own sake because to experience it is the main goal. For instance, if I played a game of chess primarily to enjoy the game, that game would be an autotelic experience for me; whereas if I played for money, or to achieve a competitive ranking in the chess world, the same game would be primarily *exotelic*, that is, motivated by an outside goal. Applied to personality, autotelic denotes an individual who generally does things for their own sake, rather than in order to achieve some later external goal.

Of course no one is fully autotelic, because we all have to do things even if we don't enjoy them, either out of a sense of duty or necessity. But there is a gradation, ranging from individuals who almost never feel that what they do is worth doing for its own sake, to others who feel that most anything they do is important and valuable in its own right. It is to these latter individuals that the term autotelic applies.

An autotelic person needs few material possessions and little entertainment, comfort, power, or fame because so much of what he or she does is already rewarding. Because such persons experience flow in work, in family life, when interacting with people, when eating, and even when alone with nothing to do, they are less dependent on the external rewards that keep others motivated to go on with a life composed of dull and meaningless routines. They are more autonomous and independent, because they cannot be as easily manipulated with threats or rewards from the outside. At the same time, they are more involved with everything around them because they are fully immersed in the current of life.

But how can one find out if someone is autotelic? The best method is to observe a person over a long period of time, in many different situations. A short "test" of the kind psychologists use is not very appropriate, in part because flow is such a subjective experience that it would be relatively easy for a person to fake his or her responses. A prolonged interview or questionnaire may help, but I prefer to use a more indirect measure. According to the theory, persons should be in flow when they perceive both the challenges in a given situation and their skills to be high. So one way of measuring how autotelic a person is, is by computing the frequency with which they report being in a high-challenge, high-skill situation over a week of paging with the Experience Sampling Method. We find that there are people who report being in this situation over 70 percent of the time, and others less than 10 percent. We assume that the former are more autotelic than the latter.

Using this method, we can look at what distinguishes peo-

Figure 4.1
Percentage of Time Spent in Various Activities by Autotelic Teenagers

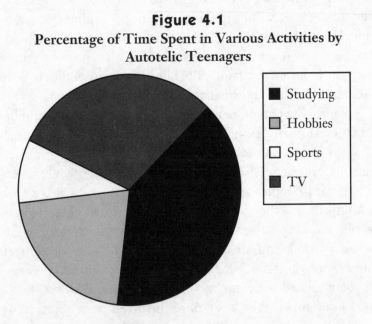

Source: Adapted from Adlai-Gail 1994.

Figure 4.2
**Percentage of Time Spent in Various Activities by
Non-Autotelic Teenagers**

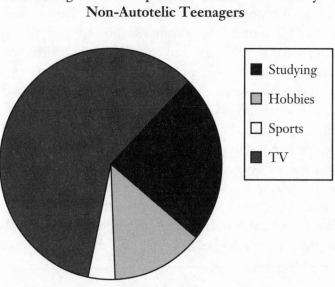

Studying

Hobbies

Sports

TV

Source: Adapted from Adlai-Gail 1994.

ple whose experiences are mainly autotelic from those who
rarely experience this state. For instance, in one study we
took a group of two hundred very talented teenagers, and divided them into two groups: fifty whose frequency of high-
challenges, high-skill responses during the week was in the
upper quartile (the "autotelic" group), and contrasted them
with fifty who were in the lower quartile (the "non-autotelic"
group). Then we asked the question: Are these two groups of
adolescents using their time in different ways? The most significant contrasts between the two groups are shown in figures 4.1 and 4.2. Each autotelic teenager spent on the
average 11 percent of waking time studying, which is 5 percentage points more than a teen in the other group spent.
Because each percentage point is roughly equivalent to one
hour, we can say that in a week the autotelic teens spent
eleven hours studying, the others six.

The other differences involve hobbies, where the first

group spent almost twice the amount of time (6 versus 3.5 percent), and sports (2.5 versus 1 percent). The one reversal is in terms of time spent watching television: the non-autotelic watched TV almost twice as often as the autotelic (15.2 versus 8.5 percent). Very similar and equally significant results were found in a later study of a representative sample of American adolescents, where 202 autotelic teenagers were compared to 202 non-autotelic ones. Clearly an important dimension of what it means to be autotelic is what one does with one's time. Passive leisure and entertainment do not provide much opportunity to exercise one's skills. One learns to experience flow by getting involved in activities that are more suited to provide it, namely, mental work and active leisure.

But is the quality of experience of autotelic youngsters better than that of their peers? After all, the fact that they do more

Figure 5.1
Quality of Experience Over a Week of ESM Sampling for 202 Autotelic and 202 Non-Autotelic Adolescents When Involved in Productive Activities

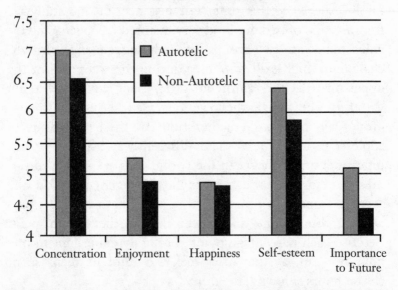

Source: Adapted from Hektner 1996.

challenging things is in part true by definition, since we defined being autotelic as being often in challenging situations. The real question is whether being often in flow-producing situations actually improves subjective experience. The answer is yes. To illustrate the results, figure 5.1 presents the average weekly responses of the two groups of 202 autotelic and 202 non-autotelic teenagers representative of the national high school population, when they are doing either academic or paid work. The results show that when involved in productive activities, the first group concentrates significantly more, has a significantly higher self-esteem, and sees what they are doing as very significantly more important for their future goals. However, the two groups are not significantly different in terms of enjoyment or happiness.

How about the quality of experience in active leisure? Figure 5.2 shows the pattern of differences. First of all, as one

Figure 5.2
Quality of Experience Over a Week of ESM Sampling for 202 Autotelic and 202 Non-Autotelic Adolescents When Involved in Active Leisure

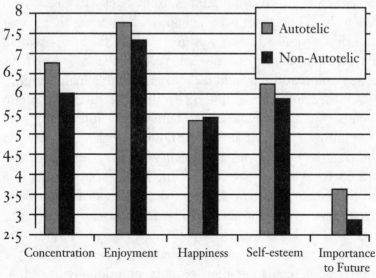

Source: Adapted from Hektner 1996 and Bidwell et al. 1997, in press.

would expect, in leisure all teens report higher enjoyment and happiness than they do in productive activities; however, they concentrate less and feel that what they do is less important for their future goals. The comparisons between the groups, except for happiness, are all statistically significant. Autotelic youngsters concentrate more, enjoy themselves more, have higher self-esteem, and see what they do as more related to their future goals. All of this fits what we would expect, except for one thing. Why aren't they happier?

What I have learned from decades of doing research with the ESM is that self-reported happiness is not a very good indicator of the quality of a person's life. Some people say they are "happy" even when they dislike their jobs, when their home life is nonexistent, when they spend all their time in meaningless activities. We are resilient creatures, and apparently we are able to avoid feeling sad even when all the conditions suggest otherwise. If we can't say we are at least somewhat happy, what's the point of going on? Autotelic persons are not necessarily happier, but they are involved in more complex activities, and they feel better about themselves as a result. It is not enough to be happy to have an excellent life. The point is to be happy while doing things that stretch our skills, that help us grow and fulfill our potential. This is especially true in the early years: A teenager who feels happy doing nothing is unlikely to grow into a happy adult.

Another interesting finding is that the autotelic group spends a significantly higher amount of time interacting with the family—on the order of four hours a week—compared to the others. This begins to explain why they learn to enjoy more whatever they are doing. The family seems to act as a protective environment where a child can experiment in relative security, without having to be self-conscious and worry about being defensive or competitive. American child rearing has emphasized early independence as a central goal: the sooner adolescents left their parents, emotionally as well as physically, the earlier they were supposed to mature. But early maturity is not such a great idea. Left to fend for themselves too early, young people can easily become insecure and defensive. It could be argued, in fact, that the more complex the adult world in which they have to find a place, the longer a period of dependence an adolescent needs in order to prepare for it. Of course this "social neoteny" only works if the family is a relatively complex unit that provides stimulation as well as support; it would not help a child to stay dependent on a dysfunctional family.

If there is one quality that distinguishes autotelic individuals, it is that their psychic energy seems inexhaustible. Even though they have no greater attentional capacity than anyone else, they pay more attention to what happens around them, they notice more, and they are willing to invest more attention in things for their own sake without expecting an immediate return. Most of us hoard attention carefully. We dole it out only for serious things, for things that matter; we only get interested in whatever will promote our welfare. The objects most worthy of our psychic energy are ourselves and the people and things that will give us some material or emotional advantage. The result is that we don't have much attention left over to participate in the world on its own terms, to be surprised, to learn new things, to empathize, to grow beyond the limits set by our self-centeredness.

Autotelic persons are less concerned with themselves, and therefore have more free psychic energy to experience life with. Kelly, one of the teenagers in our study who usually reports high challenges and high skills on her ESM forms, differs from her classmates in that she is not thinking most of the time about boyfriends, shopping at the mall, or how to get good grades. Instead she is fascinated by mythology and calls herself a "Celtic scholar." She works in a museum three afternoons a week, helping to store and classify artifacts. She enjoys even the most routine aspects of her work, like "putting everything in cubbyholes and things like that," as well as being alert to what is going on around her and learning from it. At the same time she enjoys her friends, with whom she has long debates about religion and life after school. This does not mean that she is altruistic or self-effacing. Her interests are still expressions of her unique individuality, but she seems to genuinely care for what she does at least in part for its own sake.

Creative individuals are usually autotelic as well, and they often achieve their breakthroughs because they have surplus psychic energy to invest in apparently trivial objects. The neuropsychologist Brenda Milner describes the attitude she has toward work, which is shared by other scientists or artists at the frontiers of their field: "I would say I am impartial about what is important or great, because every new little discovery, even a tiny one, is exciting at the moment of discovery." The historian Natalie Davis explains how she chooses the problems to work on: "Well, I just get really curious about some problem. It just hooks in very deeply. . . . At the time, it just seems terribly interesting. . . . I may not know what is personally invested in it, other than my curiosity and my delight."

The inventor Frank Offner, who after perfecting jet engines and EEG machines, at age eighty-one became interested in studying the physiology of hair cells, gives a perfect example of the humility of autotelic individuals confronting the mysteries of life, even the seemingly most insignificant ones:

> Oh, I love to solve problems. If it is why our dishwasher does not work, or why the automobile does not work, or how the nerve works, or anything. Now I am working with Peter on how the hair cells work, and ah . . . it is so very interesting. . . . I don't care what kind of problem it is. If I can solve it, it is fun. It is really a lot of fun to solve problems, isn't it? Isn't that what's interesting in life?

This last quote also suggests that the interest of an autotelic person is not entirely passive and contemplative. It also involves an attempt to understand, or, in the case of the inventor, to solve problems. The important point is that the interest be *disinterested*; in other words, that it not be entirely at the service of one's own agenda. Only if attention is to a certain extent free of personal goals and ambitions do we have a chance of apprehending reality in its own terms.

Some people seem to have had this surplus attention available to them very early in life, and used it to wonder about everything within their ken. The inventor Jacob Rabinow saw his first automobile when he was seven years old, as he was growing up in a Chinese provincial town. He remembers immediately crawling under the car, to see how the wheels were turned by the engine, and then going home to carve a transmission and differential gears out of wood. Linus Pauling describes his childhood in terms typical of most creative individuals:

> When I was 11 years old, well, first I liked to read. And I read many books . . . when I was just turning 9 . . . [I] had already read the Bible and Darwin's *Origin of Species*. And . . . when I was 12 and had a course in ancient history in high school—first year—I enjoyed reading this textbook so that by the first few weeks of the year had read through the whole textbook and was looking around for other material about the ancient world. When I was 11, I began collecting insects and reading books in entomology. When I was 12, I made an effort to collect minerals. I found some agates—that was about all I could find and recognize in the Willamette Valley—but I read books on mineralogy and copied tables of properties, hardness and color and streak and other properties of the minerals out of the books. And then when I was 13 I became interested in chemistry. I was very excited when I realized that chemists could convert certain substances into other substances

with quite different properties. . . . Hydrogen and oxygen gases forming water. Or sodium and chlorine forming sodium chloride. Quite different substances from the elements that combined to form the compounds. So ever since then, I have spent much of my time trying better to understand chemistry. And this means really to understand the world, the nature of the universe.

It is important to notice that Pauling was not a child prodigy who astonished his elders with intellectual brilliance. He pursued his interests on his own, without recognition and little support. What started him on a long and productive life was a determination to participate as fully as possible in the life around him. Hazel Henderson, who has devoted her adult life to starting organizations for the protection of the environment, such as Citizens for Clean Air, describes vividly the attitude of joyous interest such people share:

When I was five—you know, like where you just open your eyes and look around and say, "Wow, what an incredible trip this is! What the hell is going on? What am I supposed to be doing here?" I've had that question in me all my life. And I love it! It makes every day very fresh. . . . And then every morning you wake up and it's like the dawn of creation.

But not everyone is fortunate to have as much free psychic energy as Pauling or Henderson. Most of us have learned to save up our attention to cope with the immediate demands of living, and have little of it left over to be interested in the nature of the universe, our place in the cosmos, or in anything else that will not register as a gain on our ledger of immediate goals. Yet without disinterested interest life is uninteresting. There is no room in it for wonder, novelty, surprise, for transcending the limits imposed by our fears and prejudices.

If one has failed to develop curiosity and interest in the early years, it is a good idea to acquire them now, before it is too late to improve the quality of life.

To do so is fairly easy in principle, but more difficult in practice. Yet it is sure worth trying. The first step is to develop the habit of doing whatever needs to be done with concentrated attention, with skill rather than inertia. Even the most routine tasks, like washing dishes, dressing, or mowing the lawn become more rewarding if we approach them with the care it would take to make a work of art. The next step is to transfer some psychic energy each day from tasks that we don't like doing, or from passive leisure, into something we never did before, or something we enjoy doing but don't do often enough because it seems too much trouble. There are literally millions of potentially interesting things in the world to see, to do, to learn about. But they don't become actually interesting until we devote attention to them.

Many people will say that this advice is useless to them, because they already have so many demands on their time that they absolutely cannot afford to do anything new or interesting. Time stress has become one of the most popular complaints of the day. But more often than not, it is an excuse for not taking control of our lives. How many of the things that we do are really necessary? How many of the demands could be reduced if we put some energy into prioritizing, organizing, and streamlining the routines that now fritter away our attention? It is true that if we let time run through our fingers we will soon have none left. One must learn to husband it carefully, not so much in order to achieve wealth and security in some distant future, but in order to enjoy life in the here and now.

Time is what one must find in order to develop interest and curiosity to enjoy life for its own sake. The other equally important resource is the ability to control psychic energy. Instead of waiting for an external stimulus or challenge to grab our attention, we must learn to concentrate it more or less at will. This ability is related to interest by a feedback loop of mutual causation and reinforcement. If you are interested in something you will focus on it, and if you focus attention on anything, it is likely that you will become interested in it.

Many of the things we find interesting are not so by nature, but because we took the trouble of paying attention to them. Until one starts to collect them, insects and minerals are not very appealing. Nor are most people until we find out about their lives and thoughts. Running marathons or climbing mountains, the game of bridge or Racine's dramas are rather boring except to those who have invested enough attention to realize their intricate complexity. As one focuses on any segment of reality, a potentially infinite range of opportunities for action—physical, mental, or emotional—is revealed for our skills to engage with. There is never a good excuse for being bored.

To control attention means to control experience, and therefore the quality of life. Information reaches consciousness only when we attend to it. Attention acts as a filter between outside events and our experience of them. How much stress we experience depends more on how well we control attention, than on what happens to us. The effect of physical pain, of a monetary loss, of a social snub depends on how much attention we pay to it, how much room we allow for it in consciousness. The more psychic energy we invest in a painful event, the more real it becomes, and the more entropy it introduces in consciousness. To deny, repress, or misinterpret such events is no solution either, because the information will keep smoldering in the recesses of the mind, draining away psychic energy to keep it from spreading. It is better to look suffering straight in the eye, acknowledge and respect its presence, and then get busy as soon as possible focusing on things *we* choose to focus on.

In a study of people who became severely handicapped by disease or by accidents—blind or paraplegic—Professor

Fausto Massimini and his team found that several had adapted remarkably to their tragedy, and claimed that their lives had become better as a result of their handicap. What distinguished such individuals is that they decided to master their limitation through an unprecedented discipline of their psychic energy. They learned to derive flow from the simplest skills like dressing, walking around the house, and driving a car. Those who did best went far beyond just negotiating again the basic tasks of life. One became a swimming instructor, others became accountants, traveled to play at international chess tournaments and swimming meets, or became archery champions shooting from a wheelchair.

The same ability to transform a tragic situation into at least a tolerable one is shown by victims of terrorists who survive solitary confinement or prisoners in concentration camps. In such conditions the outside, "real" environment is so barren and dehumanizing as to induce despair in most people. Those who survive are able to ignore selectively the external conditions, and to redirect their attention to an inner life that is real only to themselves. It is easier to do so if you know poetry, mathematics, or some other system of symbols that allows you to concentrate and do mental work without any visible, material props.

These examples suggest what one needs to learn to control attention. In principle any skill or discipline one can master on one's own will serve: meditation and prayer if one is so inclined; exercise, aerobics, martial arts for those who prefer concentrating on physical skills. Any specialization or expertise that one finds enjoyable and where one can improve one's knowledge over time. The important thing, however, is the attitude toward these disciplines. If one prays in order to be holy, or exercises to develop strong pectoral muscles, or learns to be knowledgeable, then a great deal of the benefit is lost. The important thing is to enjoy the activity for its own sake, and to know that what matters is not the result, but the control one is acquiring over one's attention.

Normally, attention is directed by genetic instructions, so-cial conventions, and habits we learned as children. There-fore it is not we who decide what to become aware of, what information will reach consciousness. As a result, our lives are not ours in any meaningful sense; most of what we expe-rience will have been programmed for us. We learn what is supposed to be worth seeing, what is not; what to remember and what to forget; what to feel when we see a bat, a flag, or a person who worships God by different rites; we learn what is supposed to be worth living and dying for. Through the years, our experience will follow the script written by biology and culture. The only way to take over the ownership of life is by learning to direct psychic energy in line with our own intentions.

The Love of Fate

Whether we like it or not, our lives will leave a mark on the universe. Each person's birth makes ripples that expand in the social environment: parents, siblings, relatives, and friends are affected by it, and as we grow up our actions leave a myriad of consequences, some intended, most not. Our consumer decisions make a tiny difference in the economy, political decisions affect the future of the community, and each kind or mean act modifies slightly the total quality of human well-being. Persons whose lives are autotelic help to reduce entropy in the consciousness of those who come in contact with them; those who devote all their psychic energy to competing for resources and to aggrandizing their own self add to the sum total of entropy.

One cannot lead a life that is truly excellent without feeling that one belongs to something greater and more permanent than oneself. This is one conclusion that is common to all the various religions that have given meaning to people's lives all through the long epochs of human history. Nowadays, still heady from the great advances brought about by science and technology, we are in danger of forgetting this insight. In the United States and the other technologically advanced societies, individualism and materialism have almost completely prevailed over allegiance to the community and to spiritual values.

It is significant that Dr. Benjamin Spock, whose advice about child rearing was so immensely influential among at least two generations of parents, in the twilight of his life doubts that the stress placed earlier on training children to be unfettered individualists was such a good idea. He now feels that it is at least as essential for them to learn to work for a common good, and to appreciate religion, art, and the other ineffable aspects of life.

In fact, the warning signs that we have become too enamored of ourselves are many. An example is the inability of people to form commitments, which has resulted in half the urban population in developed countries spending their lives alone, and in the dissolution of such a high proportion of marriages. Another is the increasing disillusionment that people report, in survey after survey, with most of the institutions that we had previously trusted, and with the individuals who lead them.

More and more, we seem to bury our heads in the sand to avoid hearing bad news, withdrawing into gated communities protected by armed response. But a good personal life is impossible while staying aloof of a corrupt society, as Socrates knew and those who have lived under recent dictatorships have found out. It would be so much easier if we were responsible only for ourselves. Unfortunately, things don't work that way. An active responsibility for the rest of humankind, and for the world of which we are a part, is a necessary ingredient of a good life.

The real challenge, however, is to reduce entropy in one's surroundings without increasing it in one's consciousness. The Buddhists have a good piece of advice as to how this can be done: "Act always as if the future of the Universe depended on what you did, while laughing at yourself for thinking that whatever you do makes any difference." It is this serious playfulness, this combination of concern and humility, that makes it possible to be both engaged and carefree at the same time. With this attitude one does not need to win to feel content; helping to maintain order in the universe becomes its own reward, regardless of consequences. Then it is possible to find joy even when fighting a losing battle in a good cause.

A first step out of this impasse is to gain a clearer understanding of one's self—the image each person develops about who he or she is. We couldn't get very far without a self. But the downside of the self-image is that as soon as it emerges in early childhood, it begins to control the rest of consciousness. Because we identify ourselves with it, believing it to be the central essence of our being, the self increasingly appears to be not only the most important among the contents of consciousness, but—at least for some people—the only one worth paying attention to. The danger is that one's entire psychic energy will go toward satisfying the needs of the imaginary entity we have ourselves created. This might not be too bad, if the self we bring into being is a reasonable entity. But children who are abused may grow up constructing a hopeless, or vindictive, image of self; children who are indulged without being loved may create narcissistic selves. A self may grow to be insatiable, or have a completely exaggerated idea of its importance. Persons who own such a distorted self nevertheless feel compelled to satisfy its needs. If they think they need more power, or money, or love, or adventure, they will do everything to satisfy that need even beyond what is good for them in the long run. In such cases a person's psychic energy, directed by an ill-conceived ego, is likely to cause entropy in the environment as well as within consciousness.

Being without a sense of self, an animal will exert itself until its biological needs are satisfied, but not much further. It will attack a prey, defend its territory, fight for a mate, but when these imperatives are taken care of, it will rest. If, however, a man develops a self-image based on power, or wealth, there are no limits to his exertions. He will pursue the goal set by the self relentlessly, even if he has to ruin his health in the process, even if he has to destroy other people along the way.

It is not so surprising, then, that so many religions have blamed the ego for being the cause of human unhappiness. The radical advice is to neuter the ego by not allowing it to dictate desires. If we refuse to heed our needs by giving up food, sex, and all the vanities that men strive for, the ego will eventually have no say in what to do, and will shrivel and die. But there is no way to completely do away with the ego and still survive. The only viable alternative is to follow a less radical course, and make sure that one gets to know one's self, and understands its peculiarities. It is then possible to separate those needs that really help us to navigate through life, from those malignant growths that sprout from them and make our lives miserable.

When asked what has been the most difficult obstacle to overcome in his career, the novelist Richard Stern answered:

I think it's that rubbishy part of myself, that part which is described by such words as vanity, pride, the sense of not being treated as I should be, comparison with others, and so on. I've tried rather hard to discipline that. And I've been lucky that there has been enough that's positive to enable me to counter a kind of biliousness and resentment . . . which I've seen paralyze colleagues of mine, peers who are more gifted than I. I've felt it in myself. And I've had to learn to counter that.

I would say that the chief obstacle is—oneself.

For each of us, the chief obstacle to a good life is oneself. Yet if we learn to live with it, and like Ulysses find a way to resist the siren song of its needs, the self can become a friend, a helper, a rock upon which to build a fulfilling life. Stern goes on to describe how, as a writer, he can tame the unbridled ego and make it do creative work:

> Of course there are things in myself . . . which I know are bad, mean, twisted, weak, this, that, or the other thing. I can draw strength from that. . . . I can transform them. They're sources of strength. And as I said earlier, the writer takes those, and they're his material.

One need not be an artist to transform the "rubbishy parts" of the self into a deeper understanding of the human condition. We all have the opportunity to use ambition, the need to be loved—even aggressiveness—in constructive ways, without being carried away by them. Once we realize what our demons are, we need not fear them any longer. Instead of taking them seriously, we can smile with compassion at the arrogance of these fruits of our imagination. We don't have to feed their ravenous hunger except on our own terms, when to do so helps us achieve something worthwhile.

Of course, this is easier said than done. Ever since the Delphic oracle started giving the sensible advice "Know thyself" some three thousand years ago, people who thought about these things agreed that one must first come to know and then master the ego before embarking on a good life. Yet we have made very little progress in the direction of self-knowledge. All too often those who extol most loudly the virtues of selflessness turn out to be motivated by greed and ambition.

In our century, the project of self-knowledge has been most strongly identified with Freudian analysis. Shaped by the radical cynicism of the between-war years, psychoanalysis set its sights modestly: it offered self-knowledge without aspiring to tell what one should do with it once attained. And the understanding it offered, profound as it was, was also rather limited to revealing only some of the snares that the ego typically falls into—the malignancies that result from trying to cope with the family triangle and the subsequent repression of sexuality. Important as this insight has been, it had the unfortunate result of providing a false sense of security to people who believed that by exorcising some childhood trauma they would live happily ever after. The self, alas, is more cunning and complicated than that.

Psychotherapy relies primarily on recalling and then sharing past experiences with a trained analyst. This process of guided reflection can be very useful, and in its form it does not differ that much from the injunction of the Delphic oracle. The difficulty comes when the popularity of this form of therapy leads people to believe that by introspecting and ruminating upon their past they will solve their problems. This usually does not work, because the lenses through which we look at the past are distorted precisely by the kind of problems we want solved. It takes an expert therapist, or long practice, to benefit from reflection.

Moreover, the habit of rumination that our narcissistic society encourages actually might make things worse. The ESM research shows that when people think about themselves, their moods are usually negative. When a person starts to reflect without being skilled at it, the first thoughts that pop into the mind tend to be depressing. Whereas in flow we forget ourselves, in apathy, worry, and boredom the self is usually at center stage. So unless one has mastered the skill of reflection, the practice of "thinking about problems" usually aggravates whatever is wrong instead of alleviating it.

Most people only think about themselves when things are not going well, and thereby they enter a vicious circle in which present anxiety colors the past, and then the painful memories make the present even more bleak. One way to break out of this circle is to develop the habit of reflecting on one's life when there is reason to feel good about it, when one is in an upbeat mood. But it is even better to invest psychic energy in goals and relationships that bring harmony to the self indirectly. After experiencing flow in a complex interaction, the feedback is concrete and objective, and we feel better about ourselves without having had to try.

In order to experience flow, it helps to have clear goals— not because it is achieving the goals that is necessarily important, but because without a goal it is difficult to concentrate and avoid distractions. Thus a mountain climber sets as her goal to reach the summit not because she has some deep desire to reach it, but because the goal makes the experience of climbing possible. If it were not for the summit, the climb would become pointless ambling that leaves one restless and apathetic.

There is quite extensive evidence showing that even if one does not experience flow, just the fact of doing something in line with one's goals improves the state of mind. For example, being with friends is usually uplifting, especially if we see that interacting with friends is what we want to do at the moment; but if we feel we should be working, then the time spent with the same friends is much less positive. Conversely even a disliked job makes us feel better if we manage to see it as part of our goals.

These findings suggest that a simple way of improving the quality of life is to take ownership of one's actions. A great deal of what we do (over two-thirds, on the average) are things we feel we have to do, or we do because there isn't anything else we feel like doing. Many people spend their entire lives feeling like puppets who move only because their strings are pulled. Under these conditions we are likely to feel that our psychic energy is wasted. So the question is, why don't we *want* to do more things? The sheer act of wanting focuses attention, establishes priority in consciousness, and thus creates a sense of inner harmony.

There are many things in life that we must do and don't like doing. It may be sitting in meetings, or taking out the garbage, or keeping track of bills. Some of these are unavoidable; no matter how ingenious we are, we still must do them. So the choice is either to do them against the grain, grumbling about the imposition—or do them willingly. In both cases we are stuck with having to do the activity, but in the second case the experience is bound to be more positive. One can set goals for even the most despised task: for instance, to mow the lawn as quickly and efficiently as possible. The very act of setting the goal will take much of the sting out of a chore.

This attitude toward one's choices is well expressed in the concept of *amor fati*—or love of fate—a central concept in Nietzsche's philosophy. For instance, in discussing what it takes to live fully, he writes: "My formula for greatness in a human being is *amor fati:* That one wants nothing to be different, not forward, not backward, not in all eternity. . . . Not merely bear what is necessary . . . but love it." And: "I want to learn more and more to see as beautiful what is necessary in things; then I shall be one of those who make things beautiful."

Abraham Maslow's studies led him to similar conclusions. Based on his clinical observations and interviews with individuals he considered to be self-actualizing, including creative artists and scientists, he concluded that the processes of growth resulted in fulfilling peak experiences. These involved a consistency between self and environment; and he referred to this as harmony between "inner requiredness" and "outer requiredness," or between "I want" and "I must." When this happens, "one freely, happily, and wholeheartedly embraces one's determinants. One chooses and wills one's fate."

The psychologist Carl Rogers also endorsed a very similar perspective. He comments about what he calls the fully functioning person: "He wills or chooses to follow the course of action which is the most economical vector in relation to all the internal and external stimuli because it is that behavior which will be the most deeply satisfying." As a result, he continues: "The fully functioning person . . . not only experiences, but utilizes, the most absolute freedom when he spontaneously, freely, and voluntarily chooses and wills that which is absolutely determined." Thus, as with Nietzsche and Maslow, the love of fate corresponds to a willingness to accept ownership of one's actions, whether these are spontaneous or imposed from the outside. It is this acceptance that leads to personal growth, and provides the feeling of serene enjoyment which removes the burden of entropy from everyday life.

The quality of life is much improved if we learn to love what we have to do—in this Nietzsche and company were absolutely right. But in retrospect one can begin to see the limitations of the "humanistic psychology" of which Maslow and Rogers were such outstanding leaders. In the glory days of the mid-century, when prosperity reigned and peace beckoned around the corner, it made sense to assume that personal fulfillment could only lead to positive outcomes. There was no need then to make invidious comparisons about ways of fulfilling oneself, to question whether one set of goals was better than another—what mattered was to do one's thing. The optimistic haze blunted all edges, and we permitted ourselves to believe that the only evil came from not fulfilling one's potential.

The problem is that people also learn to love things that are destructive to themselves and to others. Teenagers arrested for vandalism or robbery often have no other motivation than the excitement they experience stealing a car or breaking into a house. Veterans say that they never felt such intense flow as when they were behind a machine gun on the front lines. When the physicist Robert J. Oppenheimer was developing the atomic bomb, he wrote with lyrical passion about the "sweet problem" he was trying to solve. From all accounts, Adolph Eichmann enjoyed working on the logistic problems involved in transporting Jews to extermination camps. The moral implication of these examples is clearly different, but they make the point that enjoying what one does is not a sufficient reason for doing it.

Flow is a source of psychic energy in that it focuses attention and motivates action. Like other forms of energy, it is neutral—it can be used for constructive or destructive purposes. Fire can be used to warm us up on a cold night or it can be used to burn down the house. The same is true of electricity or nuclear energy. Making energy available for human use is an important accomplishment, but learning how to use it well is at least as essential. Thus in creating a good life it is not enough to strive for enjoyable goals, but also to choose goals that will reduce the sum total of entropy in the world.

So where is one to find such goals? It has been the task of religions to define entropy as it applies to human affairs. It was called "sin," and it consisted in behavior that harmed the person, the community, or its values. All societies that have survived have had to define positive goals to direct the energy of their people; to make them effective, they created supernatural beings who communicated the rules of right and wrong behavior through visions, apparitions, and texts dictated to special individuals like Moses, Mohammed, or Joseph Smith. These goals could not be justified only in terms of our lives here and now, because if the only effects of our actions were the ones we could observe in this life, common sense would dictate that we get as much pleasure and material advantage as we can, even if we must be ruthless in the process. Yet a community would be destroyed if everyone was motivated by sheer selfishness, so all religions had to provide a scenario for what happens to those who act only in terms of self-interest—such as being reincarnated in a lower form of life, or being forgotten, or going to hell.

One of the main challenges of our time is to discover new bases for transcendent goals that fit with whatever else we know about the world. A new myth to give meaning to life, if you will, but one that will serve us for the present and the near future—just as earlier myths have helped our ancestors to make sense of their existence, relying on the images, metaphors, and facts known to them. But just as the elements of past myths were believed to be true to those who used them, we have also to believe in the truth of this new dispensation.

In the past, it was the prophets who voiced the myths that gave power to the beliefs of the community. Drawing on familiar images, they intimated that a supreme being was speaking through them to tell the people how they should behave, and what the world beyond our senses was like. There may still be prophets in the future claiming to know such things, but it is less likely that they will be believed. One consequence of depending on science for solving material problems and on democracy for solving political conflicts is that we have learned to distrust the vision of a single individual, no matter how inspired. Of course, the "cult of personality" is still very much alive, but it is more tempered by healthy skepticism. A credible revelation would have to have that element of consensus we have come to expect from scientific truth, and from democratic decision making.

Instead of waiting for prophets, we may discover the foundations on which to build a good life from the knowledge scientists and other thinkers are slowly accumulating. There are enough hints about how the universe functions to know what kind of actions support the increase of complexity and order, and what kind lead toward destruction. We are rediscovering how all forms of life depend on each other and on the environment. How precisely each action produces an equal reaction. How difficult it is to create order and useful energy, and how easy it is to waste it in disorder. We learn that the consequences of actions may not be immediately visible, but may have effects in distant connections, because everything that exists is part of an interconnected system. Much of this has been already said, in one way or another, in the religions of the Plains Indian tribes, the Buddhists, the Zoroastrians, and innumerable other beliefs based on a careful observation of life. What contemporary science adds is a systematic expression of these facts in a language that has authority in our times.

But there are also other, perhaps more exciting insights latent in modern science. For instance, the implications of relativity might suggest a way to reconcile the monotheistic beliefs that have been so successful in the last two millennia, and the more fragmented, idiosyncratic polytheistic forms they replaced. The disadvantage of polytheism has been that when people actually believed in the existence of separate spirits, demiurges, demons, and gods, each with its own character and sphere of authority, it caused a great deal of confusion and dissipation of attention among the competing spiritual entities. The postulate of a single God, whether by the Israelites, the Christians, or the Muslims, reordered the believers' consciousness, releasing a tremendous amount of psychic energy, which swept other faiths aside. However, the downside of monotheism was that by specifying a single supreme being it tended to develop into rigid dogmatism.

What relativity and the more recent discoveries about fractal geometries may suggest is that the same reality may be packaged in different bundles, so to speak, and that depending on the perspective of the viewer, the angle of vision, the time frame, and the scale of observation one might see very different pictures of the same underlying truth. Thus there is no need to brand as heresy visions and insights that differ from the beliefs we learned as children, yet we also know that these are locally valid, temporary manifestations of a single underlying process of enormous complexity.

Many of the relevant strands converge around the process of evolution. Ironically, while Darwin's observations were justly seen as a threat to fundamentalist Christian religion, the idea that over very long periods of time ecological systems and the structure of organisms tend toward increasing complexity has given hope to several scientists that the universe is not ruled by chaos, but conceals a meaningful story. One of the earliest to express this connection was the Jesuit paleontologist Pierre Teilhard de Chardin, whose *The Phenomenon of Man* gave a lyrical—and perhaps excessively lyrical—description of evolution from atomic dust billions of years ago to the unification of mind and spirit in what he called the Omega Point, his equivalent for the traditional concept of souls joining with the supreme being in heaven.

Teilhard's vision was derided by most scientists, but some of the more adventurous ones—such as C. H. Waddington, Julian Huxley, and Theodosius Dobzhansky—took it rather seriously. In one form or other, evolving complexity has the making of a myth robust enough to hang a faith on. For instance, Jonas Salk, the inventor of the polio vaccine—who saw himself to be as much an artist and a humanist as a scientist—spent the last years of his life struggling to understand how past life may hold the key to the future. In his words:

I have continued to be interested in some . . . more fundamental questions, about creativity itself. . . . I see us as a product of the process of evolution, I would say creative evolution. We have now become the process itself, or part of the process itself. And so from that perspective I have become interested in universal evolution, the phenomenon of evolution in itself as manifest in what I call pre-biological evolution, evolution of the physical, chemical world; biological evolution; and meta-biological evolution of the brain-mind. And now I'm beginning to write about what I call teleological evolution, which is evolution with a purpose. So my purpose now, you might say, is to try to understand evolution, creativity, in a purposeful way.

It is too soon to see clearly what lies beyond these new horizons that are just opening up. But writers and scientists are beginning to piece together the vision that might lead into the future. Some of these efforts still seem so fanciful as to be part only of the realm of imagination. For instance, Madeleine L'Engle has woven into her novels for children plots where events in the cells of the body parallel historical struggles among human characters, which in turn reflect cosmic conflicts between supernatural beings. And she is perfectly aware that the science fiction she writes has ethical consequences. Even when the characters in the book suffer and are about to be engulfed by the forces of evil, she believes that: "You have to get them out, into some kind of hope. I don't like hopeless books. Books that make you think, 'Ah, life's not worth living.' I want to leave them thinking, yeah, this endeavor is difficult, but it is worth it, and it is ultimately joyful."

John Archibald Wheeler, one of the most distinguished physicists of this century, spends his time puzzling about how we play a vital part in bringing about the material world that seems to exist objectively outside and apart from ourselves. Benjamin Spock, the eminent pediatrician, is trying to redefine spirituality in terms that make sense for our times. And then there are those who, like the economist and activist Hazel Henderson, have adopted a joyously free-form personal philosophy in which their identity is seen as a momentary embodiment of the ongoing stream of life:

> On one level I feel like an extraterrestrial. I'm here visiting for a while. And I'm also in human form. I'm very emotionally attached to the species. And so I have incarnated myself at this time. But I also have an infinite aspect to myself. It all kind of hangs together quite easily for me. It sounds flippant, but the thing is that this is a spiritual practice for me.

It may seem that such pagan exuberance is nothing more than a return to past superstitions, on a par with belief in reincarnation, alien abductions, or extrasensory perception. The essential difference is that New Age believers take their faith literally, while the people I am quoting know that they are speaking metaphorically, using approximations to an underlying reality they believe in, but cannot express adequately. They would be the last to reify their insights, believing them to be literally true. They know that their knowledge is itself evolving, and in a few years might have to be expressed in entirely different terms.

It is one thing for evolution to help us envision the future with reference to the past, and another to give us directions for creating a meaningful, satisfying existence. Surely, one of the reasons traditional religions have had such a powerful hold on human consciousness is that they personalized cosmic forces—for instance, by claiming that God created us in His image, thus making it possible for thousands of Christian painters to represent Him as a benign old patriarch. And perhaps more importantly, they lent each individual's life a dignity and the promise of eternity. This is indeed a hard act to follow. The process of evolution as we understand it now works statistically on large numbers, and has nothing to say about individuals; it is run by determinism coupled with chance instead of purpose and free will. Thus it appears to be an arid doctrine with no chance to inspire a person to organize his or her life with reference to it.

Yet the findings of science may have hopeful things to say to each of us. In the first place, they make us increasingly aware of how unique each person is. Not only in the particular way the ingredients of the genetic code have been combined, yielding instructions for developing unprecedented physical and mental traits. But also unique in the time and the place in which this particular organism has been set to encounter life. Because an individual becomes a person only within a physical, social, and cultural context, when and where we happen to be born defines a single coordinate of existence that no one else shares.

Thus each of us is responsible for one particular point in

space and time in which our body and mind forms a link within the total network of existence. For whereas it is true that who we are is determined by genetic instructions and social interactions, it is also true that having invented the concept of freedom, we can make choices that will determine the future shape of the network of which we are a part. What kind of cosmetics we use will help determine whether the air will stay fit to breathe, how much time we spend talking to teachers will affect what our children learn, and the kind of shows we watch will influence the nature of commercial entertainment.

Contemporary understanding of matter and energy also suggests a new way of thinking about good and evil. Evil in human affairs is analogous to the process of entropy in the material universe. We call evil that which causes pain, suffering, disorder in the psyche or the community. It usually involves taking the course of least resistance, or operating according to the principles of a lower order of organization. For instance, when a person endowed with consciousness acts in terms of instincts alone, or when a social being acts selfishly even though the situation calls for cooperation. When scientists work on perfecting means of destruction they are succumbing to entropy even if they use the latest and most sophisticated knowledge. Entropy or evil is the default state, the condition to which systems return unless work is done to prevent it.

What prevents it is what we call "good"—actions that preserve order while preventing rigidity, that are informed by the needs of the most evolved systems. Acts that take into account the future, the common good, the emotional well-being of others. Good is the creative overcoming of inertia, the energy that leads to the evolution of human consciousness. To act in terms of new principles of organization is always more difficult, and requires more effort and energy. The ability to do so is what has been known as virtue.

But why should one be virtuous when it is so much easier

to let entropy prevail? Why should one want to support evo-lution without the promise of eternal life as a reward? If what we have said so far is true, eternal life is actually part of the package of existence—not in the way cartoons represent the afterlife, with haloed characters in nightgowns standing around on clouds, but in the fact that our actions in this life are going to reverberate through time and shape the evolving future. Whether our present consciousness of individuality is preserved in some dimension of existence after death or dis-appears completely, the unalterable fact is that our being will forever remain part of the warp and woof of what is. The more psychic energy we invest in the future of life, the more we become a part of it. Those who identify with evolution blend their consciousness with it, like a tiny creek joining an immense river, whose currents become as one.

Hell in this scenario is simply the separation of the indi-vidual from the flow of life. It is clinging to the past, to the self, to the safety of inertia. There is a trace of this sense in the root of the word for "devil": it comes from the Greek *dia bollein*, to separate or break asunder. What is diabolical is to weaken the emerging complexity by withdrawing one's psy-chic energy from it.

Of course, this is not the only way to read what science implies about the future. It is also possible to see nothing but meaningless chance at work in the world, and be discouraged by it. In fact, it is easier to do so. Entropy holds also for how we interpret the evidence of the senses. But this chapter started with the question: How can we find a goal that will allow us to enjoy life while being responsible to others? Choosing this interpretation for the current knowledge sci-ence provides might be one answer to that question. Within an evolutionary framework, we can focus consciousness on the tasks of everyday life in the knowledge that when we act in the fullness of the flow experience, we are also building a bridge to the future of our universe.

☰NOTES

Chapter 1

1. **Auden.** An excellent set of reflections on Auden's poetry and on its place in contemporary literature are in Hecht (1993).

4. **Systematic phenomenology.** The theoretical and empirical bases for the claims made in this volume can be found, for instance, in Csikszentmihalyi (1990, 1993); Csikszentmihalyi and Csikszentmihalyi (1988); Csikszentmihalyi and Rathunde (1993).

5. **Baboons.** A detailed description of the activities of free-ranging primates is given in Altmann (1980). The daily activities of peasants in the south of France during the Middle Ages are reported in Le Roy Ladurie (1979).

6. **Differences in daily life.** The French historians associated with the review *Annales* pioneered the study of how ordinary people lived in different historical periods. An example of the genre is Davis and Farge (1993).

8. **E. P. Thompson.** Thompson (1963) gives some of the most vivid descriptions of how daily life changed as a result of industrialization in England.

9. **Table 1.** The sources for the data presented in this table are

as follows: the time budget of American adults, using the ESM, has been reported in Csikszentmihalyi and Graef (1980); Csikszentmihalyi and LeFevre (1989); Kubey and Csikszentmihalyi (1990); Larson and Richards (1994); for that of adolescents see Bidwell et al. (in press); Csikszentmihalyi and Larson (1984); Csikszentmihalyi, Rathunde, and Whalen (1993).

9. **Time budgets.** How much time hunter-gatherers spent in productive activities has been estimated by Marshall Sahlins (1972). Similar results are also reported in Lee and DeVore (1968). For time budgets in the eighteenth century see Thompson (1963), and in recent times Szalai (1965).

11. **Women carried water . . .** The quote is from Hufton (1993, p. 30).

12. **Leisure.** For a detailed history of leisure, see Kelly (1982).

13. **Cultures differ . . .** McKim Marriot describes the traditional Hindu view of the individual's position in the social context (Marriott 1976); for the comparison of Caucasian and East Asian children see Asakawa (1996).

14. **The public sphere.** The argument about the importance of having a public sphere for the development of individuality was made by Hannah Arendt (1956).

15. **The Experience Sampling Method.** Those who might be interested in the details of this method should consult Csikszentmihalyi and Larson (1987); Moneta and Csikszentmihalyi (1996).

Chapter 2

18. **Nine basic emotions.** The main emotions that can be differentiated and that are recognized across cultures are joy, anger, sadness, fear, interest, shame, guilt, envy, and depression (Campos and Barrett 1984).

18. **Genetically wired emotions.** Although Charles Darwin himself realized that emotions served survival purposes and evolved just like physical organs of the body did, it was not until very recently that psychological traits began to be studied from an evolutionary perspective. A recent example is the work of David Buss (1994).

19. **Happiness.** One of the first modern psychological studies of happiness, *The Structure of Psychological Well-Being* by Norman Bradburn (1969), originally had the word "happiness" in its title, but this was later changed to "psychological well-being" to avoid seeming unscientific. Current studies include the extensive summary of the topic by Myers (1992), the work by Myers and Diener (1995), and Diener and Diener (1996), which finds that people are generally happy; another source is Lykken and Tellegen (1996). The international comparisons of income and happiness are in Inglehart (1990). The main problem is that such studies are based on respondents' global assessments of their own happiness. Because people are strongly biased to see their own life as happy regardless of its content, such a measure does not give much information about the quality of a person's life.

22. **Psychic entropy or conflict in consciousness,** and its opposite, psychic negentropy, which describes states of inner harmony, are described in Csikszentmihalyi (1988, 1990); Csikszentmihalyi and Csikszentmihalyi (1988); Csikszentmihalyi and Rathunde (in press).

23. **Self-esteem.** William James' formula for self-esteem was published in James (1890). The contrast in self-esteem between ethnic groups is in Asakawa (1996) and Bidwell et al. (in press). The self-esteem differences between mothers who are working and at home was studied by Ann Wells (1988).

25. **Mental operations.** I discussed the role of attention in thinking in Csikszentmihalyi (1993). The Yale psychologist Jerome Singer has studied daydreaming extensively (J. L. Singer 1966, 1981).

27. **Varieties of intelligence.** The canonical work in this field is Howard Gardner's analysis of the seven main forms taken by human intelligence (Gardner 1983).

27. **The development of talent.** The effort it takes to develop a young person's talent is described in studies by Benjamin Bloom (1985), and those I conducted with my students (Csikszentmihalyi, Rathunde, and Whalen 1993).

29. **The flow experience.** Some of the main sources dealing with this experience are Csikszentmihalyi (1975, 1990); Csikszentmihalyi and Csikszentmihalyi (1988); Moneta and Csik-

szentmihalyi (1996). For more specialized studies, see also Adlai-Gail (1994); Choe (1995); Heine (1996); Hektner (1996); Inghilleri (1995). "Optimal experience" and "psychic negentropy" are sometimes used interchangeably for the flow experience.

30. **Figure 1.** The sources for this figure are in Csikszentmihalyi (1990) and Massimini and Carli (1988). This representation has gone through several revisions over the years, as empirical findings forced us to revise our initial hypotheses. For instance, the most recent revision has involved the reversal in the placement of the experiences of "relaxation" and "boredom." Originally I had thought that low challenges and high skills must result in the experience of boredom. However, many studies, e.g. Adlai-Gail (1994), Csikszentmihalyi and Csikszentmihalyi (1988), and Hektner (1996), show that people report feeling relaxed in such a situation, whereas boredom tends to occur more when both challenges and skills are low.

33. **How often in flow?** The large survey of flow among Germans is reported in Noelle-Neumann (1995). Some interesting accounts of flow in different activities are the following: writing, Perry (1996); computers, Trevino and Trevino (1992), Webster and Martocchio (1993); teaching, Coleman (1994); reading, McQuillan and Conde (1996); management, Loubris, Crous, and Schepers (1995); sports, Jackson (1996), Stein, Kimiecik, Daniels, and Jackson (1995); gardening, Reigberg (1995) among others.

Chapter 3

40. **Psychopathology and flow.** The psychiatrist Marten De Vries (1992) has been one of the first to investigate in close detail how psychiatric patients actually feel, and discovered in the process several counterintuitive findings about psychopathology. For the work of Professor Massimini and his group at the University of Milan see Inghilleri (1995); Massimini and Inghilleri (1986).

41. **Creative people.** The quote from Richard Stern and those that will follow later in this volume are taken from my recent

study of creativity (Csikszentmihalyi 1996), which is based on interviews with ninety-one artists, scientists, political and business leaders who have changed the culture in which we live to some extent. On the relationship between flow and creativity, see also the collection edited by George Klein (1990).

41. **Solitude.** For the deleterious effects of being alone, see, for instance, Csikszentmihalyi and Larson (1984); Larson and Csikszentmihalyi (1978); Larson, Mannell, and Zuzanek (1986).

43. **National survey** findings that indicate a link between happiness and having friends were reported by Burt (1986).

43. **Experience in the family.** The recent study by Reed Larson and Maryse Richards, in which all members of the family participated in an ESM study at the same time (Larson and Richards 1994), reveals many intriguing patterns in family experience: as the title of their book, *Divergent Realities*, implies, parents and children are rarely on the same page when they interact at home.

44. **Driving a car.** That driving is one of the most enjoyable experiences in many people's lives was suggested by one of our ESM studies (Csikszentmihalyi and LeFevre 1989); a more in-depth ESM study sponsored by Nissan USA revealed many unanticipated details, some of which are reported throughout this volume.

45. **Surroundings and their psychological effects.** For an exception to the general neglect of how our surroundings affect emotions and thoughts see Gallagher (1993). Other work on this topic includes Csikszentmihalyi and Rochberg-Halton (1981).

46. **Time of the week and physical symptoms.** Two unpublished pilot studies, one completed by Maria Wong at the University of Michigan and the other by Cynthia Hedricks (in press) at the University of Southern California, find that significantly more physical symptoms are reported on Sundays, as well as in situations that do not require focused attention, suggesting that being occupied to a certain extent prevents us from noticing pain.

Chapter 4

49. **Americans want to work.** These survey results are from Yankelovich (1981), and they have been replicated by similar patterns in other countries. For the ambivalence about work see Csikszentmihalyi and LeFevre (1989); and the dialogue between the German social scientists is in Noelle-Neumann and Strumpel (1984). Noelle-Neumann interpreted the link between willingness to work and a positive lifestyle as evidence that "work makes you happy," whereas Strumpel understood the general preference for leisure to mean that "work makes you unhappy."

50 **The history of work.** For some interesting insights as to how work has changed over the centuries see, for instance, Braudel (1985); Lee and DeVore (1968); Norberg (1993); Veyne (1987).

53. **Table 3.** Results concerning how American teenagers learn attitudes and skills relevant to their future occupations were obtained in the course of a five-year longitudinal study of almost four thousand students in middle and high school across the United States, which was sponsored by the Sloan Foundation (Bidwell et al. 1992). The negative experiences associated with activities that are neither like work nor like play were explored in detail by Jennifer Schmidt (1997).

56. **Women and work.** Gender differences in the experience of work are reported in Larson and Richards (1994). Anne Wells (1988) found the differences in self-esteem between mothers who worked full time and part time.

58. **Unemployment.** ESM studies of unemployed youth in the United Kingdom were conducted by John Haworth (Haworth and Ducker 1991). The international survey studies of unemployment are reported in Inglehart (1990).

Chapter 5

64. **Leisure is dangerous.** The psychiatrists' warning was reported in *Psychiatry* (1958); for similar arguments see Gussen (1967); Kubey and Csikszentmihalyi (1990).

65. **Sunday neurosis.** The reference is in Ferenczi (1950); see also Boyer (1955); Cattell (1955).

69. **Reading books.** The differences found between individuals who were frequent readers and those who were frequent TV viewers are reported in Noelle-Neumann (1996).

70. **Herodotus.** See *Persian Wars*, Book 1, Chapter 94.

71. **Leisure and cultural decline.** For some of the historical evidence see Kelly (1982); some of the current cross-cultural material is in Inghilleri (1993).

72. **Leisure-centered lives.** The study by Macbeth is reported in Macbeth (1988); the quote from the ocean sailor is in Pirsig (1977); that from the rock climber is in Csikszentmihalyi (1975).

76. **Energy use and leisure.** The finding that the use of nonrenewable energy in leisure is negatively related to happiness, at least for women, is reported in Graef et al. (1981).

Chapter 6

78. **Therapeutic effects of companions.** The reference is to the work of Lewinsohn (1982).

79. **Non-Western emphasis on the social context.** The importance of belonging to a social network in India is discussed by Hart (1992); Kakar (1978); Marriott (1976); in Japan by Asakawa (1996); Lebra (1976); Markus and Kitayama (1991).

81. **Friends.** For the importance of friendship to a satisfying life see Myers (1992).

84. **Sexuality.** How selective forces throughout evolution have shaped our sexual emotions, attitudes, and behaviors is well described in Buss (1994). For a cultural history of human sexuality see I. Singer (1966). The exploitation of sexuality is discussed in Marcuse (1955).

85. **Family.** The composition of families in the Middle Ages is described in Le Roy Ladurie (1979). Other forms of family arrangements are discussed in Edwards (1969); Herlihy (1985); Mitterauer and Sieder (1982).

88. **Moods in the family.** These findings are from the research, already mentioned several times, by Larson and Richards (1994).

88. **Complex families.** The theoretical notion of complexity was applied to the family system by Kevin Rathunde (in press). See also Carroll, Schneider, and Csikszentmihalyi (1996); Csikszentmihalyi and Rathunde (1993); Csikszentmihalyi and Rathunde (in press); Huang (1996) for other findings that use this concept.

89. **Sorcery and solitude.** The generalized paranoia of the Dobuans is described by Reo Fortune ([1932] 1963). The concept of conversation as a means of reality maintenance was developed by the sociologists Peter Berger and Thomas Luckman (1967).

90. **Preference for solitary scenery.** The survey in question is reported in Noelle-Neumann and Kocher (1993, p. 504).

91. **Talent and solitude.** Data that show how students who cannot stand being alone have trouble developing their talents is presented in Csikszentmihalyi, Rathunde, and Whalen (1993).

92. **Fear of strangers.** The French historian Philippe Aries described the dangers incurred by medieval students in Paris (Aries, 1962). The threat to women walking the streets in the seventeenth century is mentioned by Norberg (1993).

93. *Vita activa.* Hannah Arendt (1956) discusses the difference in worldviews implied by an active as against a contemplative life. The distinction between "inner-directed" and "outer-directed" ways of life appeared in Riesman, Glazer, and Denney (1950). The typology of "extroversion" versus "introversion" was developed by Carl Jung (1954); for its current measurement, see Costa and McCrae (1984).

94. **Extroverts happier.** Research suggesting that extroverts tend to be more satisfied with their lives is reported by Myers (1992).

Chapter 7

98. **Fifteen percent of the population.** For this figure, see last note to Chapter 2.

98. **Gramsci.** A very readable biography of this Italian political theorist is by Fiore (1973).

100. **Frequency of flow.** The study reported here was done by Joel Hektner (1996).

101. **Why jobs are resented.** The ideas mentioned in this section largely derive from the many years of counseling with business managers that I carried out with the University of Chicago summer extension program in Vail, Colorado.

102. **Lives dedicated to others.** The biographies of individuals with exceptional moral sensitivity were collected and analyzed by Colby and Damon (1992).

103. **Making jobs more meaningful.** One of the earliest and still most insightful accounts of how workers who are proud of their jobs think is the series of interviews collected by Studs Terkel (1974).

106. **Stress and strain.** The physiologist Hans Selye was the first to identify "eustress," or the positive value of manageable stress for the organism. The optimal psychological response to strain is widely investigated (Selye 1956).

112. **Flow in relationships.** The quote describing a mother's enjoyment when playing with her child comes from Allison and Duncan (1988).

Chapter 8

116. **To be totally absorbed . . .** The quote is from Allison and Duncan (1988).

123. **Social neoteny.** In embryology, "neoteny" refers to the retardation of development in human infants as compared to other primates and mammal species. This is supposed to allow for more learning to occur as the nervous system matures in interaction with the environment rather than in the isolation of the womb (Lerner 1984). Social neoteny is an extension of this concept to the tendency for some young people to benefit from a longer period of maturation protected within the family (Csikszentmihalyi and Rathunde in press).

128. **Attention.** The importance of controlling attention, or "psychic energy," is fundamental to taking charge of one's life. Some of the thinking relevant to this claim can be found in Csikszentmihalyi (1978, 1993).

128. Blind and paraplegic. Fausto Massimini and his team at the
University of Milan have interviewed a great number of individuals struck by tragedy, such as people who have become
paraplegic, or blind (Negri, Massimini, and Delle Fave 1992).
Contrary to what one might expect, many such individuals are
able to enjoy their lives more after a tragic accident than they
did before. See also Diener and Diener (1996). Conversely,
research with lottery winners (Brickman, Coates, and Janoff-
Bulman 1978) suggests that gaining sudden financial fortune
does not improve happiness. These results confirm the old
wisdom that it is not what happens to a person that determines the quality of life, but what a person makes happen.

Chapter 9

132. Community and individuality. Some of the most important
recent statements about the lack of involvement with values
greater than the individual are by Bellah et al. (1985, 1991);
Lash (1990). For comments on the necessity to create new
values as old ones lose credibility see Massimini and Delle
Fave (1991).

133. Self and evolution. A brief description of how the self
evolves philogenetically and ontogenetically is given in Csikszentmihalyi (1993).

138. Nietzsche's concept of *amor fati* is in Nietzsche ([1882]
1974). For Maslow's thoughts on the same subject, see
Maslow (1971), and for Rogers' see Rogers (1969).

139. R. J. Oppenheimer's quote, and the problem of finding
flow in destructive activities, is discussed in Csikszentmihalyi
(1985); Csikszentmihalyi and Larson (1978).

143. Evolution. Some of the pioneers who have extended evolutionary thought to the realm of human cultural evolution
have been Bergson (1944); Campbell (1976); J. Huxley
(1947); T. H. Huxley (1894); Johnston (1984); Teilhard de
Chardin (1965).

146. Good and evil, from the viewpoint of evolutionary theory, is
discussed by Alexander (1987); Burhoe (1986); Campbell
(1975); Williams (1988).

⹋REFERENCES

Adlai-Gail, W. S. 1994. *Exploring the autotelic personality.* Ph.D. diss., University of Chicago.

Alexander, R. D. 1987. *The biology of moral systems.* New York: Aldine De Gruyter.

Allison, M. T., and M. C. Duncan. 1988. Women, work, and flow. In *Optimal Experience: Psychological studies of flow in consciousness,* edited by M. Csikszentmihalyi and I. S. Csikszentmihalyi. New York: Cambridge University Press, pp. 118–37.

Altmann, J. 1980. *Baboon mothers and infants.* Cambridge, Mass.: Harvard University Press.

Arendt, H. 1956. *The human condition.* Chicago: University of Chicago Press.

Aries, P. 1962. *Centuries of childhood.* New York: Vintage.

Asakawa, K. 1996. *The experience of interdependence and independence in the self-construal of Asian American and Caucasian American adolescents.* Ph.D. diss., University of Chicago.

Bellah, R. N., R. Madsen, W. M. Sullivan, A. Swidler, and S. M. Tipton. 1985. *Patterns of the heart.* Berkeley, Calif.: University of California Press.

———. 1991. *The good society.* New York: Alfred A. Knopf.

Berger, P. L., and T. Luckmann. 1967. *The social construction of reality.* Garden City, N.Y.: Anchor Books.

Bergson, H. 1944. *Creative evolution.* New York: The Modern Library.

Bidwell, C., M. Csikszentmihalyi, L. Hedges, and B. Schneider. In press. *Attitudes and experiences of work for American adolescents.* New York: Cambridge University Press.

———— 1992. *Studying Career Choice.* Chicago: NORC.

Bloom, B. S., ed. 1985. *Developing talent in young people.* New York: Ballantine.

Boyer, L. B. 1955. Christmas neurosis. *Journal of the American Psychoanalytic Association* 3:467–88.

Bradburn, N. 1969. *The structure of psychological well-being.* Chicago: Aldine.

Braudel, F. 1985. *The structures of everyday life.* Translated by S. Reynolds. New York: Harper and Row.

Brickman, P., D. Coates, and R. Janoff-Bulman. 1978. Lottery winners and accident victims: Is happiness relative? *Journal of Personality and Social Psychology* 36, no. 8:917–27.

Burhoe, R. W. 1986. War, peace, and religion's biocultural evolution. *Zygon* 21:439–72.

Burt, R. S. 1986. *Strangers, friends, and happiness.* GSS Technical Report No. 72. University of Chicago, NORC.

Buss, D. M. 1994. *The evolution of desire.* New York: Basic Books.

Campbell, D. T. 1975. On the conflicts between biological and social evolution and between psychology and moral tradition. *American Psychologist* 30:1103–26.

Campbell, D. T. 1976. Evolutionary epistemology. In *The Library of Living Philosophers: Karl Popper,* edited by D. A. Schlipp. La Salle, Ill.: Open Court, pp. 413–63.

Campos, J. J., and K. C. Barrett. 1984. Toward a new understanding of emotions and their development. In *Emotions, cognition, and behavior,* edited by C. E. Izard, J. Kagan, and R. B. Zajonc. Cambridge, UK: Cambridge University Press, pp. 229–63.

Carroll, M. E., B. Schneider, and M. Csikszentmihalyi. 1996. *The effects of family dynamics on adolescents' expectations.* Paper submitted for publication. The University of Chicago.

Cattell, J. P. 1955. The holiday syndrome. *Psychoanalytic Review* 42:39–43.

Choe, I. 1995. *Motivation, subjective experience, and academic achievement in Korean high school students.* Ph.D. diss., University of Chicago.

Colby, A., and W. Damon. 1992. *Some do care.* New York: The Free Press.

Coleman, L. J. 1994. Being a teacher: Emotions and optimal experience while teaching gifted children. *Gifted Child Quarterly* 38, no. 3:146–52.

Costa, P. T. J., and R. R. McCrae. 1984. Personality as a lifelong determinant of well-being. In *Emotion in adult development,* edited by C. Z. Malatesta and C. E. Izard. Newbury Park, Calif.: Sage.

Csikszentmihalyi, M. 1975. *Beyond boredom and anxiety.* San Francisco: Jossey-Bass.

———. 1978. Attention and the wholistic approach to behavior. In *The Stream of Consciousness,* edited by K. S. Pope and J. L. Singer. New York: Plenum, pp. 335–58.

———. 1985. Reflections on enjoyment. *Perspectives in Biology and Medicine* 28, no. 4:469–97.

———. 1988. Motivation and creativity: Toward a synthesis of structural and energistic approaches to cognition. *New Ideas in Psychology* 6, no. 2:159–76.

———. 1990. *Flow: The psychology of optimal experience.* New York: Harper and Row.

———. 1993. *The evolving self: A psychology for the third millennium.* New York: HarperCollins.

———. 1996. *Creativity: Flow and the psychology of discovery and invention.* New York: HarperCollins.

Csikszentmihalyi, M., and I. S. Csikszentmihalyi, eds. 1988. *Optimal experience: Psychological studies of flow in consciousness.* New York: Cambridge University Press.

Csikszentmihalyi, M., and R. Graef. 1980. The experience of freedom in daily life. *American Journal of Community Psychology* 8:401–14.

Csikszentmihalyi, M., and R. Larson. 1978. Intrinsic rewards in school crime. *Crime and delinquency* 24, no. 3:322–35.

———. 1984. *Being adolescent.* New York: Basic Books.

———. 1987. Validity and reliability of the experience sampling method. *Journal of Nervous and Mental Disease* 175, no. 9:526–36.

Csikszentmihalyi, M., and J. LeFevre. 1989. Optimal experience in work and leisure. *Journal of Personality and Social Psychology* 56, no. 5:815–22.

Csikszentmihalyi, M., and K. Rathunde. 1993. The measurement of flow in everyday life. In *Nebraska Symposium on Motivation* 40:58–97. Lincoln, Neb.: University of Nebraska Press.

———. In press. The development of the person: An experiential perspective on the ontogenesis of psychological complexity. In *Theoretical Models of Human Development*, edited by R. M. Lerner, Vol. 1, *Handbook of Child Development*. New York: Wiley.

Csikszentmihalyi, M., and E. Rochberg-Halton. 1981. *The meaning of things: Domestic symbols and the self*. New York: Cambridge University Press.

Csikszentmihalyi, M., K. Rathunde, and S. Whalen. 1993. *Talented teenagers: The roots of success and failure*. New York: Cambridge University Press.

Davis, N. Z., and A. Farge, eds. 1993. *A history of women in the West*. Cambridge, Mass.: Harvard University Press.

Delle Fave, A., and F. Massimini. 1988. The changing contexts of flow in work and leisure. In *Optimal experience: Psychological studies of flow in consciousness*, edited by M. Csikszentmihalyi and I. S. Csikszentmihalyi. New York: Cambridge University Press, pp. 193–214.

deVries, M., ed. 1992. *The experience of psychopathology*. Cambridge, UK: Cambridge University Press.

Diener, E., and C. Diener. 1996. Most people are happy. *Psychological Science* 7, no. 3:181–4.

Edwards, J. N., ed. 1969. *The family and change*. New York: Alfred A. Knopf.

Ferenczi, S. 1950. Sunday neuroses. In *Further contributions to the theory and techniques of psychoanalysis*, edited by S. Ferenczi, 174–7. London: Hogarth Press.

Fiore, G. 1973. *Antonio Gramsci: Life of a revolutionary*. New York: Schocken Books.

Fortune, R. F. [1932] 1963. *Sorcerers of Dobu*. New York: Dutton.

Gallagher, W. 1993. *The power of place: How our surroundings shape our thoughts, emotions, and actions*. New York: Poseidon Press.

Gardner, H. 1983. *Frames of mind: The theory of multiple intelligences*. New York: Basic Books.

Graef, R., S. McManama Gianinno, and M. Csikszentmihalyi. 1981. Energy consumption in leisure and perceived happiness. In *Consumers and energy conservation*, edited by J. D. Claxton et al. New York: Praeger.

Gussen, J. 1967. The psychodynamics of leisure. In *Leisure and mental health: A psychiatric viewpoint*, edited by P. A. Martin. Washington, D.C.: American Psychiatric Association.

Hart, L. M. 1992. Ritual art and the production of Hindu selves. *American Anthropological Association Meetings*. San Francisco, Calif.

Haworth, J. T., and J. Ducker. 1991. Psychological well-being and access to categories of experience in unemployed young adults. *Leisure Studies* 10:265–74.

Hecht, A. 1993. *The hidden law: The poetry of W. H. Auden*. Cambridge, Mass.: Harvard University Press.

Hedricks, C. In press. The ecology of pain in Latina and Caucasian women with metastatic breast cancer: A pilot study. In *11th Biannual meeting of the Society for Menstrual Cycle Research*, edited by J. Chrisler.

Heine, C. 1996. *Flow and achievement in mathematics*. Ph.D. diss., University of Chicago.

Hektner, J. M. 1996. *Exploring optimal personality development: A longitudinal study of adolescents*. Ph.D. diss., University of Chicago.

Herlihy, D. 1985. *Medieval households*. Cambridge, Mass.: Harvard University Press.

Huang, M. P.-L. 1996. *Family context and social development in adolescence*. Ph.D. diss., University of Chicago.

Hufton, O. 1993. Women, work, and family. In *A history of women in the West*, edited by N. Zemon Davis and A. Farge. Cambridge, Mass.: Harvard University Press, pp. 15–45.

Huxley, J. 1947. *Evolution and ethics*. London: Pilot Press.

Huxley, T. H. 1894. *Evolution and ethics and other essays*. New York: Appleton.

Inghilleri, P. 1993. Selezione psicologica bi-culturale: Verso l'aumento della complessità individuale e sociale. Il caso dei Navajo. In *La selezione psicologica umana*, edited by F. Massimini and P. Inghilleri. Milan: Cooperative Libraria Iulm.

Inghilleri, P. 1995. *Esperienza soggettiva, personalità, evoluzione culturale*. Turin, Italy: UTET.

Inglehart, R. 1990. *Culture shift in advanced industrial society.* Princeton: Princeton University Press.

Jackson, S. A. In press. Toward a conceptual understanding of the flow experience in elite athletes. *Research quarterly for exercise and sport.*

James, W. 1890. *Principles of psychology.* New York: Henry Holt.

Johnston, C. M. 1984. *The creative imperative: Human growth and planetary evolution.* Berkeley, Calif.: Celestial Arts.

Jung, C. G. 1954. *The development of personality.* New York: Pantheon.

Kakar, S. 1978. *The inner world: A psychoanalytic study of childhood and society in India.* New Delhi: Oxford University Press.

Kelly, J. R. 1982. *Leisure.* Englewood Cliffs, N.J.: Prentice-Hall.

Klein, G., ed. 1990. *Om kreativitet och flow.* Stockholm, Sweden: Brombergs.

Kubey, R., and M. Csikszentmihalyi. 1990. *Television and the quality of life.* Hillsdale, N.J.: Lawrence Erlbaum.

Larson, R., and M. Csikszentmihalyi. 1978. Experiential correlates of solitude in adolescence. *Journal of Personality* 46, no. 4:677–93.

Larson, R., and M. H. Richards. 1994. *Divergent realities: The emotional lives of mothers, fathers, and adolescents.* New York: Basic Books.

Larson, R., R. Mannell, and J. Zuzanek. 1986. Daily well-being of older adults with family and friends. *Psychology and Aging* 12:117–26.

Lash, C. 1990. *The true and only heaven: Progress and its critics.* New York: Norton.

Le Roy Ladurie, E. 1979. *Montaillou.* New York: Vintage.

Lebra, T. S. 1976. *Japanese patterns of behavior.* Honolulu: University of Hawaii Press.

Lee, R. B., and I. DeVore, eds. 1968. *Man the hunter.* Chicago: Aldine.

Lerner, R. M. 1984. *On the nature of human plasticity.* New York: Cambridge University Press.

Lewinsohn, P. M. 1982. Behavioral therapy: Clinical applications. In *Short-term therapies for depression,* edited by A. J. Rush. New York: Guilford.

Loubris, S., F. Crous, and J. M. Schepers. 1995. Management by objectives in relation to optimal experience in the workplace. *Journal of Industrial Psychology* 21, no. 2:12–17.

Lykken, D., and A. Tellegen. 1996. Happiness is a stochastic phenomenon. *Psychological Science* 7, no. 3:186–9.

Macbeth, J. 1988. Ocean cruising. In *Optimal experience: Psychological studies of flow in consciousness*, edited by M. Csikszentmihalyi and I. S. Csikszentmihalyi. New York: Cambridge University Press, pp. 214–31.

Marcuse, H. 1955. *Eros and civilisation*. Boston: Beacon.

Markus, H. R., and S. Kitayama. 1991. Culture and self: Implications for cognition, emotion, and motivation. *Psychological Review* 98, no. 2:224–53.

Marriott, M. 1976. Hindu transactions: Diversity without dualism. In *Transaction and meaning: Directions in the anthropology of exchange and symbolic behavior*, edited by B. Kepferer. Philadelphia: ISHI Publications.

Maslow, A. 1971. *The farther reaches of human nature*. New York: Viking.

Massimini, F., and M. Carli. 1988. The systematic assessment of flow in daily experience. In *Optimal experience: Psychological studies of flow in consciousness*, edited by M. Csikszentmihalyi and I. S. Csikszentmihalyi. New York: Cambridge University Press, pp. 266–87.

Massimini, F., and A. Delle Fave. 1991. Religion and cultural evolution. *Zygon* 16, no. 1:27–48.

Massimini, F., and P. Inghilleri, eds. 1986. *L'esperienza quotidiana: Teoria e metodi d'analisi*. Milan: Franco Angeli.

McQuillan, J., and G. Conde. 1996. The conditions of flow in reading: Two studies of optimal experience. *Reading Psychology* 17:109–35.

Mitterauer, M., and R. Sieder. 1982. *The European family*. Chicago: University of Chicago Press.

Moneta, G. B., and M. Csikszentmihalyi. 1996. The effect of perceived challenges and skills on the quality of subjective experience. *Journal of Personality* 64, no. 2:275–310.

Myers, D. G. 1992. *The Pursuit of Happiness*. New York: Morrow.

Myers, D. G., and E. Diener. 1995. Who is happy? *Psychological Science* 6:10–19.

Negri, P., F. Massimini, and A. Delle Fave. 1992. Tema di vita e strategie adattive nei non vedenti. In *Vedere con la mente*, edited by D. Galati. Milan, Italy: Franco Angeli.

Nietzsche, F. [1882] 1974. *The gay science*. New York: Vintage.

Noelle-Neumann, E. 1995. *AWA Spring Survey*. Allensbach Institute für Demoskopie.

————. 1996. Stationen der Glücksforschung. In *Leseglück: Eine vergessene Erfahrung?*, edited by A. Bellebaum and L. Muth. Opladen: Westdeutscher Verlag, pp. 15–56.

Noelle-Neumann, E., and R. Kocher, eds. 1993. *Allensbacher Jahrbuch der Demoskopie 1984–1992*. Munich, Germany: K.G. Saur.

Noelle-Neumann, E., and B. Strumpel. 1984. *Macht Arbeit Krank? Macht Arbeit glüchlich?* Münich: Pieper Verlag.

Norberg, K. 1993. Prostitutes. In *A history of women in the West*, edited by N. Zemon Davis and A. Farge. Cambridge, Mass.: Harvard University Press, pp. 458–74.

Perry, S. K. 1996. *When time stops: How creative writers experience entry into the flow state*. Ph.D. diss., The Fielding Institute.

Pirsig, R. 1977. Cruising blues and their cure. *Esquire* 87, no. 5:65–8.

Psychiatry, Group for the Advancement of. 1958. *The psychiatrists' interest in leisure-time activities*, no. 39.

Rathunde, K. In press. Family context and talented adolescents' optimal experience in productive activities. *Journal of research in adolescence*.

Reigberg, D. 1995. *Glück in Garten—Erfolg im Markt*. Offenburg, Germany: Senator Verlag.

Riesman, D., N. Glazer, and R. Denney. 1950. *The lonely crowd*. New York: Doubleday.

Rogers, C. 1969. *Freedom to learn*. Columbus, Ohio: Charles Merrill.

Sahlins, M. D. 1972. *Stone Age economics*. Chicago: Aldine Press.

Schmidt, J. 1997. Workers and players: Exploring involvement levels and experience of adolescents in work and play. Meetings of the *American Educational Research Association*. Boston, Mass.

Selye, H. 1956. *The stress of life*. New York: McGraw-Hill.

Singer, I. 1966. *The nature of love*. 3 vols. Chicago: University of Chicago Press.

Singer, J. L. 1966. *Daydreaming: An introduction to the experimental study of inner experience.* New York: Random House.

———. 1981. *Daydreaming and fantasy.* Oxford, UK: Oxford University Press.

Stein, G. L., J. C. Kimiecik, J. Daniels, and S. A. Jackson, 1995. Psychological antecedents of flow in recreational sports. *Personality and social psychology bulletin* 21, no. 2:125–35.

Szalai, A., ed. 1965. *The use of time: Daily activities of urban and suburban populations in twelve countries.* Paris: Mouton.

Teilhard de Chardin, P. 1965. *The phenomenon of man.* New York: Harper and Row.

Terkel, S. 1974. *Working.* New York: Pantheon.

Thompson, E. P. 1963. *The making of the English working class.* New York: Viking.

Trevino L.K., and J. W. Trevino. 1992. Flow in computer-mediated communication. *Communication Research* 19, no. 5:539–73.

Veyne, P. 1987. The Roman Empire. In *From Pagan Rome to Byzantium,* edited by P. Veyne. Cambridge, Mass: The Belknap Press, pp. 5–230.

Webster, J., and J. J. Martocchio. 1993. Turning work into play: Implications for microcomputer software training. *Journal of Management* 19, no. 1:127–46.

Wells, A. 1988. Self-esteem and optimal experience. In *Optimal Experience: Psychological studies of flow in consciousness,* edited by M. Csikszentmihalyi and I. S. Csikszentmihalyi. New York: Cambridge University Press, pp. 327–41.

Williams, G. C. 1988. Huxley's "Evolution and ethics" in sociobiological perspective. *Zygon* 23, no. 4:383–407.

Yankelovich, D. 1981. New rules in American life: Searching for self-fulfillment in a world turned upside-down. *Psychology Today* 15, no. 4:35–91.

≡INDEX

Abused children, flow and, 98–100

Achievement, self-esteem and, 23–24

Actions, taking ownership of one's, 137–40

Active leisure: adolescents and, 118–20; amateurs and, 75; difficulty of enjoying, 75; experts and, 75; flow and, 39; passive leisure versus, 66–69; quality of experience in, 121–22. *See also* Exercise; Hobbies; Movies; Music making; Restaurants; Sports

Active responsibility, 132

Activities. *See* Leisure activities; Maintenance activities; Productive activities

Adolescents: attitude toward work of, 53–55; as autotelic, 118–23; concentration and,

91, 156n; destructiveness of actions of, 139; frequency of flow in, 100–101; friends and, 42, 81, 83; lack of motivation in, 55–56; leisure activities of, 66–68; locations favored by, 43–44

Age, experiences shaped by, 6–7

Alaskans: passive leisure and, 71; work and, 52

Alcohol: apathy and, 33; as poor use of leisure time, 65, 71

Allison, Maria, 112

Amish, work and leisure activities combined by, 74–75

Ancient Greece: Aristotle and, 13, 18, 50, 51; passive leisure and, 12, 70; Socrates and, 132; work and, 50

Ancient Rome: passive leisure and, 69–70; work and, 50–51